SWEET *and* SOUR

SWEET

and SOUR

JOHN O'HARA

RANDOM HOUSE • NEW YORK

First Printing
Copyright, 1953, 1954, by John O'Hara
All rights reserved under International and
Pan-American Copyright Conventions. Published
in New York by Random House, Inc., and simul-
taneously in Toronto, Canada, by Random House
of Canada, Limited.
Library of Congress Catalog Card Number: 54–9511
Manufactured in the United States of America
by H. Wolff, N. Y.
Designed by Betty Kormusis

to Winifred Wylie Gardiner

The writing of these pieces helped to keep me busy during a period of my life when I urgently needed to keep busy. In this respect I was lucky: they began to run about two weeks before my wife died, and since Jim Kerney and I had agreed that my column was to last for six months, and since I am a pro, I kept right on writing. This column and my job on *Collier's* protected my sanity.

Without being influenced by my friendship with Jim Kerney or my own selfish interest in the matter, I believe that the existence of this column speaks well for the Kerney newspapers. It cost them money, it brought in no advertising revenue, at least on the book page. I was never asked to write down to a large circulation, and I was allowed to say what I pleased. Not many newspapers in this country, or anywhere else, would let an author sound off as I have in these pieces. If I'm wrong, I'd like to see a column of this kind in every Sunday newspaper with the same circulation, or five times or ten times the circulation. It is a sad thing how often timidity affects those publishers who are in the best position to be free of it. But then most publishers have settled for caution long before they order that first tailor-made suit.

J. O'H.

Princeton, New Jersey
July, 1954

SWEET *and* SOUR

1.

The existence of this column is all the proof you need that anybody can get a job in Trenton if he tries long enough.

Back in 1929 (or maybe it was 1930; it could have been either or both), I found myself free-lancing. There are, of course, two kinds of free-lancing: voluntary, and involuntary. In my case, and at that time, I was not a volunteer. The decision had been made for me by the city editor of the New York *Daily Mirror*. I had been a night rewrite man: fast, accurate and sufficiently acquainted with the facts of life to provide readers of the tabloids with what they seemed to want (although in those days there were not so many New Yorkers who would go so far as to slap down two cents to buy it from the *Mirror*). The job paid well, the company was a rather jolly group, and at least we could say we weren't working for the *Graphic*. Man does not live by bread alone.

Indeed, man does not live by bread alone. Perhaps if I had cultivated a taste for baked goods instead of the Martini cocktail, I'd still be on the *Mirror*. But the study of the Martini as prepared at Racky's restaurant, a block from my office, was an enjoyable way to start my day, which was supposed to begin at 6 P.M. Unfortunately for journalism, although happily for my social life, the day side of the *Mirror* would be at Racky's, on their way home, just when I was on my way to work. Consequently, the crack night re-write battery of the *Mirror* was not usually fully manned until 7 P.M. And in due course they got another boy.

I hated to leave the *Mirror*. The city editor had a Pierce-Arrow roadster and wore silk shirts, and while I would have chosen a Lincoln phaeton and button-down broadcloth, the idea was the same. There was money to be made. Moreover, as I said before, we had quite a bunch of characters. Winchell was there, a striver then, who wrote Broadway and Hollywood chatter and had not yet constituted himself a one-man State Department.

Helen Nolan, easily one of the most beautiful

2.

Happy New Year.

Here it is not yet the Epiphany and already my favorite season has passed. It is still the Christmastide, but the trees have come down, the hangovers are over, and the foreseeing ones have completed their lists of people to send cards to next December, with special emphasis on the friends who sent us a card and whom we overlooked. When I was a boy in the anthracite region of Pennsylvania the trees stayed up until January 6th, Little Christmas, or the Russian Christmas it was called. In most places January 6th was a miners' holiday and since it is also the birthday of my younger sister, there was every reason to be reminded of the date.

Along about this time of year I, as a boy, would be reading my copy of *This Year's Book for Boys*. It was a curious book and I never have found another American who read it. It was an English annual, full of stories about Fuzzy-Wuzzy and the yachting at Cowes, bravely illustrated in color. I don't know why, but I always remember the caption for one full-page picture: "Thrusting aside his musket, Boy Mockett beat a roll." Boy Mockett, as I recall, was a soldier in His Majesty's Foot who had been promoted from drummer-boy. The new drummer-boy had been picked off by The Enemy (an assegai got him, I think), leaving the platoon without a Krupa, so, thrusting aside his musket, Boy Mockett beat a roll, and I suppose, Mafeking was relieved. I know I was.

I was always full of warlike thoughts at the Christmastide. This is supposed to have a terrible effect on a child, but to that I say—since this is a family newspaper—nonsense. My first machine gun, a fairly dangerous weapon which shot rubber balls and was modeled on the Gatling gun, was given me by a priest of God, a Father Sheehan. I have nothing but the kindest thoughts of Father Sheehan, a handsome, sensitive man who took the trouble to go to Schoenhut's in Philadelphia to buy a suitable present for a little boy. In later years I fired several real machine

guns, but I never got a chance to shoot at somebody
I didn't like, so Father Sheehan (R.I.P.) has nothing on his conscience. From the time I was five until
I achieved ten I pestered my family to give me a
rifle, and when I got it—an octagonal barrel .22 Win-
chester pump gun—I was the happiest boy in Schuyl-
kill County. I became a good shot, I learned to be
careful with firearms, and in due course the weapon
was handed down to one of my five younger brothers and I began to take an interest in girls.

One girl I knew—this was a considerable time
after I surrendered my rifle—got out of Bryn Mawr
summa cum laude and for some reason I'll never understand, since she was and is one of the most attractive creatures who ever drew breath, she took a
job teaching the Flathead Indians in Montana. It
meant, of course, that she could not be home for
Christmas. She probably got more presents that year
than ever before or since. One present she got eight
times was the novel *If Winter Comes*, by A. S. M.
Hutchinson, which was an enormous best seller,
thanks in part to the generosity of her friends, who
undoubtedly thought: "Poor Margaretta, out there in
Montana with nothing to read." What's more, she
was living with two other Bryn Mawr alumnae and
they also got spare copies of *If Winter Comes*. The
novel was a not-too-exciting picture of life in an English middle-class family, and I like to think of the Indians around St. Ignatius and Moise, Montana,

asking Dad at breakfast: "Could I have the top of your egg?" Rather late in the day it occurs to me that the three Bryn Mawriers could have agreed that "If winter comes we can always put Hutchinson in the fireplace."

This duplication of books at Christmas is still a problem. Two friends, knowing my fondness for automobiles, thought of just the right book for John. Although one friend lives in Locust Valley and the other not far away in Glen Cove, they couldn't have got together. The book they chose is *A Pictorial History of the Automobile,* edited by Philip Van Doren Stern. Mr. Stern and I parted company right at the beginning, in his foreword. He says his Aunt had a "beautifully built closed carriage and a two-wheeled wicker dogcart." I never knew his Aunt, but I had a dogcart and I also had a governess cart, or what non-horsemen called a basket cart. If Mr. Stern's Aunt had a wicker dogcart she must have been very doggy indeed. In later years she would have had a solid gold Cadillac.

After his solecism about dogcarts it was no surprise to me that Mr. Stern went on to commit several errors of omission, if you can commit an omission. (You can omit a commission, because it happened to me during the war.) He prints a good picture of the 1921 Mercer Raceabout, which is all right with us who live in this neck of the woods. (I almost bought a Mercer Raceabout from a girl with the tintinnabulating name of Isabel Bell.) But nowhere will you find a photograph of the Stutz Bearcat. The 1915 model, but not the Bearcat, which had the same continued cowling as the Raceabout. I looked in vain for any mention of the Paige, which had one of the earliest, if not the first, real rumble seat, including a trick top that would cover the front seat or the front and rear. Nothing is said about the Amesbury body, although time was when half the Cadillac and Packard limousines in New York had Amesbury bodies, readily identifiable by the windshield. There is no Marmon Speedster or Jordan Playboy or Wills Sainte Claire, and no picture of a Templar that I could find (or Mr. Stern could index). These were important cars, and a little digging would have uncovered them and that is why I am disappointed in this book.

It has been said that if everybody who claims he owned a Stutz Bearcat had actually owned one, the Stutz people would be in business today. Well, that's a good enough half-observation; it is faulty because it does not consider the fact that practically every Bearcat went through at least three ownerships. I knew of one Bearcat, second-hand, that became third-hand as a result of a crap game and shortly thereafter became junk as a result of a pint of whiskey. (I came within $500 of owning Mrs. Bell's yellow Mercer; she wanted $750 for it.) The Marmon, the Playboy, the Templar and the Wills Sainte Claire were just as desirable among the younger set, and just incidentally the Mercer, Marmon and Wills built beautiful town cars for the people who could afford them. And on the subject of coachwork Mr. Stern is sadly flunking. No reference to the Murray body or the body by Schutte or Derham and not a word about Voisin, who redesigned the coachwork for the Franklin, making it appear to be a water-cooled car, and in so doing created as handsome a body job as ever came out of Syracuse, New York.

Well, part of the fun of examining a book of this kind is to pick it to pieces, and I suppose I'll have some more fun when I return to it. It's like going to work on somebody else's list of favorite tunes. Or musicians. Or authors.

3.

One of the terms of the fourteen-page contract which brought this newspaper and me together is that I have to read the books I write about. This unique arrangement has its drawbacks, and if word gets about among the established book critics that I agreed to the condition, my name will be Mud. There are seventeen Mudds in the 1948 *Social Register Locater,* mostly in St. Louis, Missouri, and there are four Mudds in *Who's Who* for the same year. But no Muds, so if it is going to be my name it is going to have to be my first name. Mud O'Hara. I don't like it. It sounds too much like a dishonest prize fighter in a *Saturday Evening Post* serial. Let us therefore hope that the established book critics do not hear about my contract with the management.

This high-level type thinking can be traced to my examination of conscience over a book called *This Was Racing*, which is what is known to us in the trade as a clip book: pieces written for newspapers or magazines and collected by the author or some other admirer. In this case the author was Joe H. Palmer, and the editor is Red Smith. Joe H. Palmer wrote horse racing for the New York *Herald Tribune*. He died on October 31, 1952, and offhand I can think of only two other writing men whom I didn't know whose deaths affected me so deeply. The other men were Ring Lardner and Lloyd Lewis.

I have stood at a bar with Ring Lardner, but didn't have the nerve to introduce myself. I probably have stood at the very same bar with Joe H. Palmer, without knowing he was there. My sadness over his death was not lessened by the fact that I was going to meet him the week after he died, when he expected to be the guest of Joe Stevens right here in Princeton. (Stevens belongs to that numerous brotherhood of Yale men who believed New Haven is a nice place to visit but wouldn't live there if you gave them the place.) Joe Stevens was well acquainted with Joe Palmer because the Stevens family are caterers and concessionaires at leading ball parks and race tracks, and I gather that Joe Palmer knew how to live. More than a hint of that trait is dropped in the pieces in *This Was Racing* and for a man on the wagon the book can be fairly rough going. I mean Joe Palmer makes good living so attractive that you want to see once again what a dry martini tastes like. When I go off the wagon I am going to ask Joe Stevens to mix me the kind of martini Joe Palmer drank. You know: upon what mart did Joe Palmer feed?

The examination of conscience referred to above was not a difficult one. Most of the pieces in the book had appeared in the *Herald Tribune* and as an early Palmer fan I missed mighty few of them. But as of this writing I have not reread them all. One reason I have not reread all of them is that I had to stop to write this piece. I warn you, though: this book is going to be like that bowl of salted peanuts on a bar. You think you're going to take a few, and you know what happens.

It is always a pleasure to rediscover that it is possible to be interested in sports without being compelled to take the Moron's Oath. Joe Palmer, a native Kentuckian, started out to be a college professor, and was a college professor. They tell me he could, and often did, talk Chaucerian like a native. (A native of Chaucer, Madam.) He fulfilled all the requirements except the actual writing of his thesis for a Ph.D., then decided he wanted to cover racing.

The only practical use he put to his classical scholarship, at least that I have found, is in a paragraph about the naming of Singing Wood, which was by Royal Minstrel out of Glade. "For surely," he says, "you have not forgotten so much of your Anglo-Saxon as not to remember that 'singing wood' was an Anglo-Saxon 'kenning,' or nickname, for a harp." From now on I shall think of myself as a singing wood. You may also call me the wind in the willows. Amounts to the same thing, practically.

While we are on the subject of scholarly sports fans leave us not leave out Red Smith himself. I had the pleasure one time of putting Red up for membership in a club. You don't just call a man Red when you are putting a man up for a club. That's how I learned that the "W" in Walter W. Smith stood for Wellesley. I have not checked lately, but I believe Red is one of a very few Notre Dame graduates middle-named Wellesley. Having Wellesley as a middle name is almost like having an extra degree. Possibly Red's father and mother were tempted to call him Vassar Wellesley Smith and wouldn't that be something? Vassar Wellesley Smith, A.A., Notre Dame.

I am waiting to see what, if any, abuse Red is going to get for the following statement, which appears in a reprint of a piece he wrote after Joe Palmer died: "Joe Palmer could write better than anybody else in the world whose stuff appeared in newspapers." He will get no abuse from me, and the fact that it is Red Smith who made the statement should act as a restraint on some hotheads. But he could not have come out so unequivocally before 1939 without a squawk from here. It was in 1939 that Heywood Broun died, and I guess Broun was the best-writing newspaper man I ever knew of. Almost fifteen years after his death he can still tease Westbrook Pegler into a lip-flopping rage. But I'm no fool and I'm no liar: on the rare occasions when Pegler writes about the fight mob, the gamblers and the other charmers who were on his beat before he signed with Roy Howard, nobody can top him even today. The sad thing there is that when he does write from memory he seems to be enjoying himself, and I suspect that the rest of the time he bores himself as much as he does me, to name one. Broun could handle that Weltpolitik chance, but Pegler boots it nearly ever time, and I think one reason, maybe the big reason, is that he feels Broun needling him from a distance of fifteen years. I suppose the big difference between them is that Broun had an attitude, and Pegler has only a gripe.

Will some well-read reader kindly help me track down the aphorism that goes, approximately: "There is nothing worse than an ignorant man (writer) with a readable style"? At a dinner party last week a fellow said he had written that to Heywood Broun when he, the fellow, was seventeen years old. Well, on the way home I figured out that the fellow was seventeen in 1919, or a year or so after Broun returned from assignment as a war correspondent in France. A few years ago, while doing some research for a novel, I read most of Broun's War I dispatches, and all they were was the most readable stuff in the field. My precocious acquaintance must have formed his opinion of Broun in a hurry, although I am more inclined to believe he formed it when he was twenty-two and not seventeen. But what I really would like to hang on him is the sin of appropriating a quote without credit, or taking the credit to his own.

4.

If all goes according to plan, I should be getting a nice plug in the book section of today's *Herald Tribune*. I don't know what John Hutchens is going to say about me, but I know he is going to say something and John is a friend of twenty-five years' standing. Trustingly, confidently, and I may say respectfully, I will settle for whatever John says.

Here we have a good example of literary logrolling of the higher type. In the first of these essays I made it clear, or I hope I made it clear, that the policy in this column will be "to give my friends all the best of it and blast the incompetents I don't like."

Perhaps I should have added that when a friend writes an embarrassingly bad book, I can give him all the best of it by not mentioning him at all. I'll pretend I think he is off in Tahiti, working on a life of Gauguin, or somewhere in Italy, shooting duck from a Venetian blind. There is nothing new or particularly harmful about literary back-scratching, so long as it's done out in the open. The reader—and this applies in all criticism—can get to know fairly soon what kind of person the critic is. After that it's easy: the reader simply approaches the criticisms by saying: "Well, what's this jerk shooting off his mouth about today?" or "I wonder what literary treasure has been uncovered this morning by this brilliant, keen, searching, wise, witty, lovable man." Anyone in the habit of reading critics knows that a single critic is undependable, unless you know what Critic X likes and doesn't like and how he and his likes and dislikes match up with yours.

For example, I am a good bet to disagree practically in toto with the opinions expressed by J. Donald Adams, of *The New York Times*. Dapper Don, as he most assuredly is not known to the scribbling set, has one or two pets who were born after 1875, but not many more than one or two. I believe he admires the works of John Hersey, but for the most part he seems to wish the twentieth century had never happened—and here the damn thing is more than half over. About the only thing he and I have in common is that he too seems to like Martha's Vine-yard, but I wouldn't like it if I had to see him there. At the same time—or, you might say, on the same *Times*—there is a younger critic, Orville Prescott by name, who is trying to make Adams look like an ex-istentialist. He fails, but he tries. Some Sundays when I read J. Donald and get the feeling that this was the way it was in Jenny Lind's day, I remind myself that the next day is Monday and Orville will really take me back to the steam age. And Orville is a year younger than I am. I do not agree with a word they say and I will defend to the death my right to say it.

John Hutchens is someone else again. When I have found myself in less than complete accord with him—probably not more than once or twice a year—I don't even worry about him. It can't be anything serious. Perhaps he is brooding over his once beloved Red Sox. Mayhap Hamilton College has dropped a close one to Hobart. Or he might be suf-fering from the common cold. That's how I feel about John Hutchens.

This friendship began a couple of years before I met him, before I knew he existed. In the late twen-ties I wanted to get a job on a paper in Missoula, Montana. (Oh, I had my reasons.) So I wrote to the editor. No job, but a kindly and fairly long reply, which was and still is appreciated by this then kid reporter. A few years later I landed on the *Herald*

Tribune and I had the good luck on an assignment to meet a handsome young man from the *Times*, Hutchens by name. I told him about the kindness of the man from Missoula, also named Hutchens. "Yep," said John. "My father."

John removed himself from the New York scene to work with H. T. Parker of—need I say?—the Boston *Transcript*. When he came back to New York it was to the *Trib* and a whole page of his own in the Sunday book section, and all too infrequent reviewing on the daily. He does alone and well what it takes two or three men to do on the opposition sheet: that is, he covers the week's news of the publishing world, and for good measure he contributes a short weekly profile of an author of the moment. (It irritates *The New Yorker* to see "profile" used that way in any other publication. I will always go out of my way to irritate *The New Yorker*.) He writes about the book world with wit and grace, even when he is not writing about present company. His profiles of authors tell about the authors rather than about the interviewer. The only interviewer who could touch him in these short sketches was the late Robert van Gelder. The leather medal, by the way, goes to one of Hutchens' opposite numbers who, in chatting about Ernest Hemingway last year, said: "We miss the bloke." Well, that's what Hemingway gets for loitering. You will never find Hutchens saying he misses Hemingway or any other author, and as for referring to Hemingway as a bloke—well, I revealed above that Martin Hutchens had good manners, and class tells.

I hope the bottom is not going to drop out of the book market because of my failure today to send you scampering after something brand new I recommend. However, I have been reading *The Age of the Moguls,* by Stewart Holbrook, which I notice has been in demand at the Trenton Library. Good book, good writer, easily worth the five bucks if you have any curiosity about the Rockefellers, Carnegie, Tom Lawson, James J. Hill, Henry Clay Frick, Jim Fisk, Jay Gould, Stanford, Crocker, Huntington, Hopkins and Daniel Drew, among others. "A motley crew," Mr. Holbrook calls them. "Yet taken together they fashioned a savage and gaudy age as distinctly purple as that of imperial Rome, and infinitely more entertaining."

About thirty years ago I read a book by R. F. Dibble which had the happy title, *Strenuous Americans,* which would have fitted this book equally well. Holbrook's book sets you right down in the chew-tobacco days. Chew-tobacco, gold-head cane, lapels on the vest, spanking pair of cobs, oyster palaces and girls, girls, girls. Holbrook catches it, all right.

I am grateful to Holbrook for making me notice an important fact I never have tucked away before: the fact that so many of these men made great fortunes while they were still in their thirties. (I am awfully age-conscious because I have a birthday coming up in a couple of weeks.) We are all likely to think of those rascals as too old to have any fun, and so fat that their gold watch chains were as long as a sommelier's badge of office. Not so. Virtually all of them were in the big chips by thirty-five, and there is no doubt that many of them would have lived longer if they hadn't been so appreciative of Pommery, Chincoteagues, and other appeals to the senses. Those boys were All Boy.

5.

One way I have learned to hoard hours and days for possibly more useful and certainly more pleasant expenditure is to refrain from reading practically all books about Harry Luce's news magazine, *Time*. This rule, which I never thought of as a rule until a few minutes ago, enables me to go fishing, if I were a fisherman; to play pool, if the Nassau Club had a pool table; to assay at length the contents of army-surplus store windows; to listen to the far-off sounds of the Pennsy freights in the night; to look up people in *Who's Who*, and to do ever so many other things that may be classified as interesting and instructive.

This rule, as I said before, became a rule only after I stopped and realized that it had been my practice for years. Approximately every two years you will see an announcement in the lit'ry news columns that Jon Fungo, or somebody, has turned in the completed manuscript of his new novel *The Shogun* and that the happy publishers, whom we shall call Beechcraft and Kohler, will bring out the book on October 4th. The announcement goes on to announce (if the book news has room for it) that Jon Fungo is a graduate of the University of Wisconsin, member of Phi Beta Kappa, did some gliding at Elmira, New York, served in the Air Force in Germany after War II, worked as a reporter on the Dahlonega (Ga.) *Nugget*, is married to a lady doctor ("I have a lady, Doctor!"—remember that program?), has three children, and lives on Brooklyn Heights. This is by no means a complete dossier on Brother Fungo. I have kept in just enough to give you some idea, without prattling on about the Fungo stamp collection, the Fungo skill at badminton, the Fungo library of Bessie Smith records, the Fungo Sunday painting, the Fungo Cape Cod knockabout, the Fungo preferences in food and drink, and the color of the Fungo eyes (one brown, one green). I could very easily get carried away and tell you all, everything, about Jon Fungo, because for an author this kind of thing is what you might call finger exercise. But let us stay with the not-too-fictional publication announcement; one item I deliberately saved for the end, the big whopping climax, always goes something like this: "Mr. Fungo has been until recently associated with *Time* magazine."

That's all brother. Next case.

Only it isn't all.

In due course (a phrase I do not fully understand but like the sound of) I get a note from a Miss Teresa Gaulsworthy, of Beechcraft and Kohler. Writes Miss Gaulsworthy: "Dear John O'Hara" —(never "Mr. O'Hara," never "John," always "Dear John O'Hara")—"On October 4th we are going to be the proud parents of the new novel by Jon Fungo, whom you met one day at Inskip's garage in 1946. Jon is very anxious to have you read his novel. By the way, the title is *The Shogun.* We are therefore sending you an advance copy and we would appreciate it very much if you can send us a quote before next Monday as we wish to use it in advance publicity. By the way I have always admired *The Postman Always Rings Twice* and still consider it your best book. Cordially, T. Gaulsworthy."

Four days later at nine A.M. parcel post opens my front door, drops a package on my floor, calls out a cheery good morning, and vanishes. I finish my breakfast, for I know I am going to need all my strength in the task at hand, and go out to the kitchen and arm myself with screwdriver, claw hammer, heavy scissors, and Swiss army knife. I then attack the package and shortly after ten A.M., provided there have been no interruptions, I have the pleasure of hefting for the very first time my advance copy of *The Shogun,* by Jon Fungo.

On the dust jacket there is the inevitable photograph of Brother Fungo with a silver-banded pipe and his shirt open at the neck. It is a little hard to tell what Brother Fungo really looks like, because the camera lens apparently had been covered with a light film of chocolate sauce, and the subject has a heavy beard which he has not shaved for three days. The impression is that on the day the picture was taken Jon bore a remote but fascinating resemblance to the younger D. H. Lawrence. The photograph, of course, is the work of Mrs. Fungo, a fact which is mentioned in the Fungo biographical material "overleaf."

I shall not here attempt to reproduce the style and content of the publisher's blurb, since that field of literature has been adequately covered by other essayists. If I give you the first sentence or two you will get the idea: "Robinson Lewis, American success, driving, dynamic publisher of the fantastically powerful magazine *Man,* was taking stock. Now fifty, he was beginning to doubt the validity of his empire. Clarissa Brooks Barrymore, the woman-behind-the-scenes . . ." And so on. It is a special form of literature, blurb-writing, and the creation of it explains and justifies the popularity of the martini-on-the-rocks, consumed quickly and silently, among the fellows who earn their living that way. Whenever I tell myself that work is work, I can always remind myself that it could be tougher.

At last the moment that the author has been waiting for, the moment when his public, symbolized by me, opens the book and begins to concentrate on what is known in the trade (rather medically, I think) as front matter. Front matter includes the dedication, and all first novels are dedicated. In the case of *The Shogun* it is likely to be: "For Sally—Who Knows." Or, if Brother Fungo has been in a garrulous mood at the time of the dedication: "For S. G. F.—Wise and witty, generous and kind, who sharpened the pencils, made the coffee and kept the fires going—this book is inscribed with love."

All right. If Sal doesn't like the dedication that is a problem for the Fungo family to thrash out over on Brooklyn Heights. The chances are good that there will be nothing to thrash out.

And then we come to the paragraph which I, in my zoological fashion, call the weasel. I call it that because the late Briton Hadden, Luce's co-founder of *Time*, loved the word. He even used it as a verb: "We can weasel it," meaning that we could insult anybody we wanted to, so long as we protected ourselves from the danger of an action by somebody like the late Max Steuer, who could slam a libel suit on us and take us for all the money Mr. Harkness possessed.

I read the weasel, which has been written by Brother Fungo, with an assist from Watson, Replevin, Battledore and Shuttlecock, 120 Broadway. I discover that Robinson Lewis and Harry Luce are two other fellows and that *Man*, with its curious style and its impertinent attitude, isn't one teeny bit like *Time*. I then place the novel on a shelf and go back to a more careful study of the Arrival of the Buyers.

6.

In our previous lesson we took up the problem of how to save up our one most valuable natural resource, which is time. Strenuously resisting all temptations to pun, I revealed that I put the passing hours to more pleasurable use by skipping all novels—all books, I believe I said—about Harry Luce's news magazine.

My original intention for last Sunday's thought-provoker was to start the monograph rolling with a hundred or two words about a man who has written a novel about *Time*. Years of reading those little biographical sketches signed by one James A. Linen have supplied me with the outlines for a picture of a typical present-day *Time* writer. (When I worked there in '28 and '29 the first requirement was a degree from Yale, Princeton or Harvard, in that order. I got hired in spite of my handicap, the fact that I didn't go to college anywhere, but Yale friends of my father's had put my name on the Yale Placement Bureau list, so even I, you might say, snuck under the Yale Fence.) I thought I would create a 1954 *Time* writer and proceed from there to the treatise on the *roman à clef*, which had been my principal aim. Fortunately, for I rather liked last Sunday's blast, I had seen so much of Linen's whitewashing in public that I was able to give practically a life history of a mythical *Time* writer, and have begun to believe in him myself. That left practically no space for the *roman à clef* monograph, which becomes the topic for today.

It could be defensibly argued that every novel ever written is to some extent a *roman à clef*. To be absolutely truthful with you, as I shall try to be in all these essays, my most recent book-reading was *The Bobbsey Twins at the Ice Carnival*, by Laura Lee Hope. When the name Lee is in the middle it is impossible to tell whether the lady author was born a Lee and married a Hope, or her full maiden name is Laura Lee Hope, as in Richmond, Virginia. With the limited time at hand I have investigated and found that she is not related to my good friends the

Rensselaer Lees, of Princeton, and I know for a fact that Authoress Hope is not related to Leslie Towne Hope, also a friend of mine, whom you know as Bob. And I doubt very much if she is kin to one-time columnist-author Edward Hope, the first man I ever knew to have a Brooks shirt monogrammed. My doubts about any relationship there are based on the knowledge that Edward Hope's full name was Edward Hope Coffey. Presumably he dropped the Coffey because his predecessor as conductor of The Lantern in the *Herald Tribune* was Don Marquis, whose name is forever associated with quite another beverage. Authoress Hope, for all I know, may be bussin' cousin to Anthony Hope, who wrote *The Prisoner of Zenda,* but there again we run into a little trouble, for Sir Anthony Hope's real name was Hawkins. It all makes me begin to wonder a bit about the name Laura Lee Hope. Maybe it isn't her square moniker. What if she is like, say, authoress Mary O'Hara, who wrote the Flicka stories? Authoress O'Hara's legit name is Alsop. No O'Hara ever changed his name to Alsop, you may be sure. But there we begin to get into a subject that a book could be written about, and I most certainly have no intention of writing a book about it. Therefore let us just pretend that the real name is Laura Lee Hope and discuss her work in terms of the *roman à clef.*

Her book *The Bobbsey Twins at the Ice Carnival,* one of many books, is action-packed. I read several chapters aloud to a young friend of mine, an ardent Hope fan, while she was soaking her hand in a salt-water solution to cure an infected scratch. The book is in twenty-five chapters, bearing such titles as "Fire," "The Red-Haired Man," "Bert's Invitation," "The Blizzard," "Strange News," "A Happy Surprise," "Aunt Sally's Legacy," "Danny Makes Trouble," "The Clown Helps," "An Adventure," "A Cold Welcome," "Flossie Meets the King," "More Mischief," and "Danger!" And more of the same, the chapter headings alone proving my contention that the book is action-packed. It is packed with so much action that it almost makes the eight O'Hara children of Mahantongo Street, Pottsville, Pennsylvania, seem like eight little models of deportment with occasional kittenish tendencies. Even today, when there are no longer any O'Haras on Mahantongo Street, I could easily obtain affidavits that such was never the case.

Well, then, imagine what life must have been like at the Lees' or the Hopes'. Assuming that just one book is a *roman à clef,* even slightly a *roman à clef,* can you imagine the pleasure in store for someone who once visited the authoress' home town? "Yes, I visited the town Laura Lee Hope came from. I was only a child, but I can distinctly recall one time when Gerald Hope—he's really Bert Bobbsey, you know—discovered the boa constrictor in his Grandfather Fairfax Lee's waders. Poor Gerald was blamed for it, till they found out it wasn't his fault at all." (I should have made clear that the Bobbsey children don't behave like a certain Mahantongo Street crowd. Bad things happen to the Bobbseys; they don't do bad things.) I can also imagine the letters Authoress Hope gets. "Dear Laura Lee: You probably have forgotten all about Nancy Culpeper that lived about a mile and an eighth out of town on the Warrenton Road. I am she. . . . Why don't you write up the time you and Tom Breckenridge got hold of a keg of corn and poured it in the baptismal font at St. James'? I laugh every time I think of that. I never see any of my old friends since I married Yancey, who is a North Carolina boy, but I often think of the good times we used to have."

Subtly, as always, I have introduced two of the problems attending the publication of the *roman à clef*. When you write a novel "more or less" based on real people, your public is going to expand, to include many, many other real people you've forgotten ever existed—a loss of memory, by the way, that never caused you the slightest discomfort. But once the novel has been published there will appear a whole army corps of volunteer memory-joggers like Nancy Culpeper. In your efforts to employ your imagination you may want to depart from Nancy's version of the keg-of-corn incident. You may want to relate that it was a bottle of gin (and a bunch of bananas, to be topical for the moment) that you and

Tom Breckenridge planted in old Fairfax Lee's
jodhpurs boots. If you do, the volunteer memory-
joggers will have at you. They are quite capable of
writing letters to the New York papers and even to
the *Saturday Review*, under the erroneous impression, in the latter case, that it has something to do
with literature. The joggers will go around the country, telling all who will listen that "That ain't the
way I heerd it." Pretty soon you will be known as a
fraud who never lived within a thousand miles of
the Warrenton Road, and you will be in a terrible
fix.

You will be in almost as terrible a fix as you can
get into if your novel has everything right. But I see
my time has run out, so more of this at another meeting.

7.

Two weeks ago tonight I was sitting and talking at the home of friends after Sunday supper. The telephone rang, it was for me. The *Times* of New York, a newspaper which we here in Trenton acknowledge to be a first-rate journal in its locality, wanted me to say something about Ernest Hemingway. As you know, unless you were locked up in solitary confinement—and if you were, please accept my congratulations on being sprung—Hemingway and his wife and a professional aeronaut were long overdue from a photographic reconnaissance of Victoria Falls, and were presumed lost. Half of what I said in my statement to the *Times* is as follows:

"Ernest Hemingway's work will be read as long as there are people around to read." The other half was too personal for me to repeat now. The rewrite man whom I spoke to was kind of disappointed at my brevity. "Is that all you want to say?" he asked. I don't know what more I could say. From where I sit it would seem I had called Hemingway a literary immortal, without spelling it out. Could it be that the pepping-up they're undergoing in West 43rd Street is costing something in dignity? If so, it's as though my aunt were suddenly to pop up at the Copacabana and lead the samba. (The aunt I have in mind is hale and hearty, and could probably do a samba after one lesson, but she wouldn't want to, that's the point. She leaves that sort of thing to those who do it better.)

Well, anyway, I read with some passing interest the tributes to Hemingway that got into print, especially those written by the chatter columnists. As Richard Watts said of himself: "I seem to be the only columnist who isn't an intimate friend of Ernest Hemingway." Watts is not really a columnist; he is a drama critic, but he has leave to become a temporary columnist for the purpose of his observation, for he turns out to be just about the only columnist, temporary or permanent, who was not able to produce a letter or cablegram that Hemingway had sent him a day or two before the accident. I don't know

how Hemingway keeps up that enormous correspondence, but I wish he'd cut it out.

Of the chatter columnists currently chattering I
now speak to three, a total which is subject to down-
ward revision without notice.

The three that I speak to remain on my list of
hello acquaintances because they happen not to
have done anything vicious to me. I'm not talking
about inaccuracies; I'm talking about viciousness.
But I'll take myself out of this discussion and I won't
even bring up the subject of the chatterers' influence
on journalism, for that was well handled some years
ago in St. Clair McKelway's profile of Walter Winchell. The reason I wish Hemingway would resist
that temptation to dash off a chit to the chatterers is
that I have ideals for him, and I want him to be
happy.

As one who never called him Papa, Pops, Heming-
stein or anything but Ernest, I squirm when he ex-
poses himself to overfamiliar gestures on the part
of his inferiors, who include not only the chatterers, but restaurateurs, Hollywood producers, society
folk, college professors, theatrical agents, dilettantes,
punchy pugs, politicians and the Lord only know
what-all. There are good people among restaurateurs, Hollywood producers, society folk, college
professors, theatrical agents, dilettantes, punchy
pugs, politicians, and all other groups, but the Big

Man has attracted more than his share of ticks. Once when I made a crack about one of the latchers-on he said: "Listen, maybe I wouldn't like your friends either." It happens that he does like a lot of my friends, because they are his too.

Don't think for an instant that I am coming out against bums. I could name you half a dozen guys who are real bums, and I like them. I ran into one a month or two ago in 21, one I hadn't seen in six or seven years. He is an international bum, whose name is a household word for bumdom. But I was glad to see him, he was glad to see me, we made false promises to get in touch with each other, and the next time we meet, maybe another six or seven years from now, if I'm still around and he hasn't been shot, we'll be just as glad to see each other. I could name you half a dozen lady bums, too, but while I am a straight-ticket Democrat, you mustn't get wrong ideas about us from certain recent developments. I have signed nothing. The kind of bums I like may make a kind of reflex pitch, but they don't mean any harm. They may want to borrow money or try to get you to write a script on speculation but they can't help that, and they would be genuinely sorry if you actually did lend them some of the ready, or plugged away on an if-money scenario.

Furthermore, as a paid-up member of the Authors Guild, the Dramatists Guild, and the Society of the Silurians, I am well aware of the writer's need of material, and material is obtained by proper study of mankind or Man (Pope). I have been able in the past to justify the hours and hours I spent getting gassed with Characters by explaining that the Characters would be processed into characters, small c, in some future short story or novel. Sometimes even Uncle Sugar will let that stick and allow some fraction of the money you spend in bums' company to be deducted as a professional expense. As a man grows older he ought to be allowed to deduct everything he spends in entertaining bums, for it is a youthful pursuit, requiring abundant physical resources. As it may, be that. My concern is for Hemingway and so much of the company he keeps.

If I could direct Hemingway's life, he might not have any fun at all, or so it would seem if so much of what gets into the public prints represents his idea of a good time. That's the trouble with having ideals for another man. Under my guidance he would visit New York once or twice every five years, dropping by to say hello to Charley Scribner and pick up a fat royalty check. He would be given a suite of rooms without telephone in some rich friend's house and a guest card at the Racquet Club. Being a gentleman, he would not entertain quite the same people in a friend's town house that he might in a hotel. And if he felt like tying one on, the Racquet Club, largely populated by gentlemen, would be the right place. (The Brook would be even better because it's smaller.) As an active *aficionado* of manly sports he would be able to talk as much as he liked about hunting and fishing, with an appreciative audience that would sit with him till midnight. Then the audience, entertained and instructed, would repair to the Hour Glass, and Hemingway would go home, get a good night's sleep, and thus be protected from the really industrious bores who run some of the restaurants he usually frequents, and from the fleas who, when Hemingway is not in town, have no one to bite but each other.

In time, say five years, and provided Hemingway has been deprived of postage stamps and access to the telegraph, he would be rid of the barnacles or, if he prefers, pilot fish. Then the Nobel people would have no excuse for passing him over in favor of a historian with an occasional neat turn of phrase.

8.

In an excellent piece in last week's *Herald Tribune Books* Gouverneur Paulding reviews Aldous Huxley's latest offering, a seventy-nine-page job called *The Doors of Perception.* Without going to the trouble of obtaining permission, I shall quote Mr. Paulding's first paragraph.

"One fine California morning," writes Paulding, "Mr. Aldous Huxley sat in his study staring at three flowers in a vase. Later he turned his attention to the bright bindings of his books on the bookshelves. Later he became engrossed in the contemplation of his gray flannel pants. It should not be imagined that the brilliant novelist of *Antic Hay* or *Point Counter Point* was merely postponing the evil moment when a man has to get down to his work. On the contrary, Mr. Huxley was earnestly working—the former trivia of storytelling, sarcasm and satire renounced—in the interest of science, psychology and religious mysticism. The distinguished author was experimenting with the effect of a drug called mescalin; he was goofed up; and all the while he observed his beautiful pants, his beautiful books and his three beautiful flowers, investigators observed the observer and a tape recorder registered his words. In *The Doors of Perception* Mr. Huxley succinctly narrates his experience."

I shall also quote part of the second paragraph: "Mescalin is the active principle of peyote, a root which the Indians of Mexico and the American Southwest have been chewing for centuries—and where did it get them? 'It changes the quality of consciousness more profoundly and yet is less toxic than any substance in the pharmacologist's repertory.'"

And of course I cannot resist quoting the attention-caller, the headline over the review, "Mr. Aldous Huxley Was All Goofed Up."

Now this is one of those times when a man like me has to reveal one of the weaknesses of self-education. For this would be just the moment to start throwing De Quincey at you. If, during those long hours tend-

ing a switchboard for the Pennsylvania Railroad or
sitting in the Buick while my father was on surgical
duty, I had read *Confessions of an English Opium
Eater* instead of *The Forsyte Saga,* I could pretend to
some erudition on the subject of junkies, English
junkies in particular. But these messages are read by
all sorts of people, from the Princeton version of the
Boston Sewing Circles to members of somewhat
more learned societies, and in the latter case at least
I am aware that some of my readers are just waiting
for me to stub my toe. Well, not this time, fellows.
Maybe next Sunday. In conversation I have often
amused myself by faking—successfully—an intimate
knowledge of books I never read, but in the case of
Confessions of an English Opium Eater I have to
rely for source material on my own work in the field.
And you will forgive me, I am almost sure, if I refer
to it as Flanders field, where the poppies grow.

My experience of tea, goof balls and all other
forms of junk is vicarious, being limited to sometimes
very close observation of musicians, actresses, actors, physicians, housewives, prostitutes, at least one
clergyman's wife, song writers, addressees of the *Social Register,* prize fighters, war veterans and others
who feel they will enjoy a stick of nepenthe. I take
no bow for taking the vow of abstinence. I'm afraid
of the stuff. Two aspirin tablets or a child's dosage
of stronger drugs will do for me, as my corps of
medics can tell you. And in the lovingly remem-

bered and not-too-distant past I was always able to get my charge out of Scotch whiskey.

During several sessions with the craythur I too have become engrossed in the contemplation of my gray flannel pants, sometimes the pleated ones, sometimes the unpleated ones. Sometimes they would be lying on the floor in a disorderly heap; more often they were encasing my handsome legs and would be the object of a somewhat exaggerated pity as I contemplated the cigarette burns I had caused. At forty-nine I still use the cuffs of my pants as an ash receiver, a practice I adopted in prep school so that the hall prefects would not find any evidence that I had been smoking.

Because I never was checked out in flower recognition I scarcely notice them. When they are in a room I am glad they are there, but I practically never comment on them, consequently they would not attract my attention, drunk or junked, even if Constance Spry herself had spent all afternoon arranging them.

Under Scotch whiskey I have been known to stare at the bindings of my own books and also some of Mr. Huxley's, but no utterances of mine during these examinations would justify setting up a tape recorder. Certainly Harper and Brothers would not care to publish my comments, consisting as they do of (a): "Gosh, that's a lot of books for a fellow my age," or (b) "Gosh, forty-eight years old and that's all I got to show for it."

There you have it: pants, plants or plots, observed under mere alcohol have never seemed a bit more beautiful than they are. All I see are bloomers, blooms and my life work, which on occasion has been characterized as one big blooming bloomer. And yet I am reluctant to start all over again and try mescalin.

Some years ago, a dozen or more, Mr. Huxley was having trouble with his eyesight. I was living in California at the time and so was Mr. Huxley. I was having no trouble with my eyesight, so the closest I ever came to Mr. Huxley was passing him in the corridor as he was leaving and I was entering the office of Mark Hellinger. Friends of mine who were having trouble with their eyesight—they were unable to see the bottom of a glass—had taken up the Huxley method of curing defective vision, which, simplified, was to stare at the sun. The treatment worked for Huxley, but one friend of mine darn near went blind. What I wonder now is how much of what Huxley sees while goofed is due to mescalin, and how much is traceable to his attempts to stare down Old Sol. Mad dogs and Englishmen, you know. I am suggesting that even if I were to hit the mescalin, maybe I wouldn't see anything but a primrose by the water's edge (which I wouldn't be able to identify), a tired pair of slacks, or a 25-cent reprint of *Butter-field 8*. I probably could get that effect with musca-tel, without bothering my apothecary for 50 c.c.'s of mescalin. The heightened effect, perhaps, is obtain-able only to those who have taken their basic train-ing in staring at the sun, which only an Englishman would think of in the first place. They'll stare at any-thing.

Huxley, as Mr. Paulding points out, was of course interested in a great deal more than his Daks full of Huxley and his Spode full of sweet peas. He was try-ing to work out some problems relating to Not-self and Otherness. Well, dear Reader, when a writer starts talking about Not-self and Otherness, your boy slips out quietly to bay at the moon. Ow-oo-oo-oo.

9.

When I first moved to Mercer County, a little more
than four years ago, I used to take my little old red
M-G and drive out around the countryside and deliberately lose myself. The object, of course, was to
familiarize myself with the highways and byways.
Now, after nearly five years, I can lose myself with
no trouble at all, without even using the M-G. (For
the information of sports-car fans I still have the
M-G, but I put it up on blocks during the winter.
An economy measure.) When I am invited to someone's house for the first time I inquire where the
hostess lives in relation to the Halcombs' to the

south, the Putnams' to the north, the Gallups' to the west. I seem not to be invited from the east; aside from an undeclinable invitation to the State Police chapter in Penns Neck and a bid to an enormous luncheon at the Forrestal Research Center, my activities, social and otherwise, have kept me on this side of U.S. 1. I once read a paper to the English Club at Rutgers, but that's another county, and I am willing to forget the incident if they will.

That system of getting acquainted with the boulevards and cowpaths by trying out strange roads is an old one of mine, and incidentally has nothing to do with the advice of certain protectors of American literature, who for twenty years have been saying, "O'Hara, get lost." Actually I have a pretty good sense of direction, and if it's a sunny day or a moonlit night, and I am carrying a watch, I'll always get home. I have been temporarily lost in Paris, Boston, London and Quakertown, Pennsylvania, but only because those cities have buildings and streets. (Possibly, too, in the case of Paris, Boston and London, because I have been the last to leave some buildings at closing time.) So I take it back: I do not lose myself; I merely go on a tour, an investigative ramble, somewhat in the manner of these very essays.

For when I rolled the parchment into the typewriter a few minutes ago I had, and still have, every intention of saying a few words about George Washington, one of my favorite men of all time.

Look up at the top of the page and see whose birth-day it is tomorrow. See? Topical.

It may seem odd, and a little bit patronizing, to say that George Washington is one of my favorite men of all time. Well, it's anything but. I began to realize how much I liked him when I was going on those solitary rides between here and the Delaware River. "I wonder how much this land has changed since Washington rode over it." And, "Washington was a little taller than I. I wonder if he got a better view than I'm getting now." And, "I wonder if Washington would recognize these hills." Time and time again he would make his presence felt, not be-cause of some monument or sign that had been placed as a reminder, but because I knew he had been there, drunk some of this water, breathed some of this air, been warmed right here by that same sun, been chilled by these same drafts.

It took quite a while for George Washington to get out from under the mantle of Fauntleroy that had been draped over him in my boyhood. I happen to believe the cherry-tree episode, up to but not includ-ing the phrasing of the confession. Unfortunately for me (and for Washington's standing), I was brought up to accept the little-prig version. Fortunately for me, I was brought up to tell the truth. The word honor meant a lot in my family, and still does, and the word of honor means just about everything. It wouldn't have been necessary for us to say, "I cannot tell a lie." Our version would have been: "I did it," and take the licking. Consequently, George Washington was rated by me a bit of a jerk—and probably a liar.

The years pass (and they will) and with no deliberate effort I put together my own portrait of Washington, only roughly similar to the Gilbert Charles Stuart reproductions that used to be on our school tablets. Sober of mien, yes, but not abstemious. Humorless, possibly, but not cold. A gentleman, of course, and in all probability an unbending one, but sure enough of himself to find it unnecessary to be a snob.

I see a vigorous man, quite capable of throwing a strike from left field or across the Rappahannock; a fox-hunting man, fond of most manly sports. And very tough. "Tell General Sullivan" (General John Sullivan, a State of Maine lawyer) "to use the bayonet. I am resolved to take Trenton," he said, when informed that wet priming had made muskets useless. "Press on, press on, boys."

At this appropriate time I have been reading *The Campaign of Princeton 1776-1777*, by Alfred Hoyt Bill. It was published by the Princeton University Press in 1948, but since we are dealing with people and events that date back about 177 years, a delay of six years in getting around to Mr. Bill's book may be excusable. I don't believe anything has occurred lately to cast doubts on the material in *The Cam-*

paign of Princeton. It is a slim volume—145 pages,
with an index—but like most books that tell the story
of military campaigning, it demands your full attention. I opened it at random and discovered that the
house in which I live is erected on land that was the
scene of some of the action hereabouts, and a stream
that contains some of my golf balls—not much more
than a Number 2 wood shot from where I sit—was
at one time of some importance during a skirmish.

But, as I say, the story of the campaign requires
uninterrupted concentration. How long since you've
tried to concentrate with two eight-year-olds spend-
ing a quiet afternoon in the next room? So instead of
putting on my Clausewitz and Mahan robe, I have
been riffling the pages of Mr. Bill's book, stopping
here and there when I spot Washington's name.

If Mr. Bill is rather mean to us Pennsylvanians for
our dilatory tactics, he also reports that Washington "said in his haste that the conduct of New Jersey
was 'infamous'." And I am inclined to think he is
right. You see, some Jerseyites—well, let's quote Mr.
Bill: "The Howe brothers proclaimed that, whereas
'several Bodies of Armed Men . . . do still continue
their opposition,' a full pardon, with the assurance of
liberty and the enjoyment of their property, would
be granted to all who, within sixty days, would
swear to 'remain in a peaceable Obedience to His
Majesty and not take up arms, nor encourage Others
to take up arms, in Opposition to his Authority.'

Hundreds of people . . . flocked to sign this oath."
But the "protection papers" were ignored by the
British, who looted and burned the just and the infamous alike. It makes me feel a little bit better
about the alleged unwarlike behavior of the Pennsylvanians, and at least G. Washington didn't call us
"infamous." After all, an ancestor of mine was one of
those Pennsylvanians, and I have enough to put up
with. Sometime let me tell you about my grandfather on Sherman's March to the Sea. It's a story I
don't tell south of Baltimore.

10.

What do you think of England, huh?

When I was a young man, two years out of my teens, and in a contemplative mood, I decided that the time had come for me to broaden my culture, to mingle with the people of the Old World, to add to my growing fund of knowledge by observing the citizens of the lands across the sea in their native habitat. Accordingly I booked passage in a transatlantic liner and sailed for those distant shores. Or, if you want to be dull and accurate about it, I got a job as a steward.

Until I made that decision to visit the Eastern

Hemisphere I had got most of my information about foreigners from books and magazines. England was largely, but not entirely, populated by vicars in buttoned gaiters and aprons (there must be some more rubrical word for aprons), by ladies in Newmarket boots, by gentlemen in deerstalkers, by toffs with monocles, by lags carrying life preservers, by fags carrying tea, by retired civil servants, by drivers of goods trains, by navvies in cap and scarf, by turf accountants in gray toppers, by callipygian barmaids (they arrived by callipygian), by titled fanciers of titled hogs, by the long in tooth, by the short of cash, and by Americans who commenced every statement with the cautious words, "I guess."

I guess I ought to add that the one thing all on that list had in common was that they were all potential murderers or murder victims, or so I believed. Homicide has always been so popular among English authors (as a literary subject, of course; not as a pastime) that I could not even look at a photograph in *The Field* without wondering who was planning to do whom in. There would be the usual picture of a top-drawer group, the scene being Scotland in August, the personnel being several members of the Buccleuch family; Captain the Honorable T. C. L. Wince, the cricketer; Mrs. Peek-Freans, of Nairobi, Kenya; Mr. Tommy Iceberg, the film producer; Lady Drummajor, of Belfast; Lord Spanner, winner at Brooklands in 1948; the traditional second gentleman from the left who is not identified, and a group of five gathered about the luncheon hamper who are not mentioned at all. To normal readers of *The Field* it would seem to be a pleasant outing of charming people, enjoying a good day's sport in the bracing air, looking fit and attractive in their tweeds and British Warms and tattered trench coats and capes and with not a care in the world even when some awkward beater takes a load of shot in his silly clavicle.

But I saw through it all.

Lady Drummajor was a drug addict. She'd first taken the nasty stuff to assuage the frightful pain that followed a hunting accident. She completely recovered from that and considered herself quite free of the morphine habit, then Drummajor himself was swept overboard and lost at Cowes, and Sheilagh (for that was her name), in an effort to forget her grief, again reached for the needle, and this time, you might say, it stuck. Unbeknownst to her, Drummajor had pledged the greater part of his inheritance, with the result that Sheilagh was left without a farthing to rub against another. Desperate for funds to pay for dope, with two boys at Eton and another at New College, Oxford, she drifted into an affair with Mr. Tommy Iceberg, who had been at Eton with Ducky Drummajor. Until then Tommy had always been regarded as the private property of Dolly Peek-Freans, one of the fabulous Williams sisters of

Cwm, Wales, whose name at one time had been linked with that of a certain Sea Lord, among others, and who also was believed by many to have been the original of the heroine of *The Snows of Kiliman-jaro,* by Mr. Ernest Hemingway. Between Dolly and Sheilagh there existed only a thinly veiled hostility.

Bobby Spanner, although a few years younger than Dolly Peek-Freans, had been in love with her from boyhood, following her about from watering place to watering place, gazing at her with the eyes of a cocker spaniel, and trying to lose himself in sport. His crack-up at Le Mans in '51 came just after Dolly's trip to Hollywood, U.S.A., with Tommy Iceberg, and the talk at White's Club was that it was Bobby himself who had tampered with the braking mechanism, clearly an effort to suicide while making it appear to be an accident. Upon being nursed back to health by Sister McFetridge (who sold accounts of her work to a penny shocker), Bobby plunged deep into the gay night life of London, and on at least one occasion a scene was narrowly averted during a chance encounter between Bobby and Iceberg at the 400 Club. Cooler heads prevailed, but young Spanner was known to have remarked that he was accepting the Buccleuchs' invitation in order to have it out with Tommy, once and for all.

Porchy Wince, twice recommended for the V.C. during the North African campaign, and the hero of

the 1936 Ashes, had no romantic interest in any of the
ladies in the Buccleuchs' house party, but a sudden
affluence that dated back only two years seemed to
lend some credence to the totally unsubstantiated ru-
mor that Porchy was the source, if not the actual author, of certain ugly items in a London scandal
sheet. No one dared make the outright accusation to
a man who had been mentioned in dispatches no
less than eight times, who had been such a batsman
as to evoke the names of Hobbs and Grace for comparison, but what else was there to think? Living in
a dismal flat in an obscure mews no more than two
years ago, Porchy was overnight transplanted to a
fully staffed house not too far from Grosvenor
Square. Often as not unable to afford bus fare in '52,
the gallant soldier now tooled about in a sleek black
Bentley. Once again he was a familiar figure in the
Royal Enclosure and, to be sure, at Lord's. From
being the object of pity, he had become, financially,
a figure to be envied, surrounded, as he was, by the
symbols of wealth and the accouterments of high
life, and these in a day when death duties and taxes
had reduced so many to a condition more closely
resembling that of the Wince of '52 than of the
Porchy of '54. To subtly searching inquiries as to the
source of this new wealth, Porchy, when deigning
to reply at all, would mutter some vague reference
to a colonial great-aunt, to a happy flyer in shares, to
mysterious uranium deposits in Manitoba. . . .

And that, my friends, is what I see when I look at a photograph in one of the high-toned English magagines. I could go on, if I liked and had the space, about the beaters and the hunt servants and the waiters in the background, without once consulting the works of Mr. D. H. Lawrence. My analysis of backstairs life would make this page a collectors' item, and might place this newspaper's mailing privileges in jeopardy, so they must wait for a lecture I may give at a $100-a-plate dinner (by invitation only) come Michaelmas. In fact, I am left with room only to say the foregoing does not really represent what I believe about England. Try me next Sunday if still interested.

11.

I have been having a hard time deciding whether to do my St. Patrick's Day piece for today or for next Sunday. When you have a name like O'Hara (O'Harra, for instance, is something like O'Hara, although personally I don't think the extra "r" does anything for it), and a job on a newspaper, you are a good bet to do at least one St. Patrick's Day piece a year. My distinguished brother Tom, who scouts the politicians for the *Herald Tribune*, was on general assignments before they turned him loose on the Democrats and Republicans.

General assignments, of course, means that one

day you go in and are told to cover the rescue of a pussycat off a flagpole; the next day you compose a thriller that has involved your attending a dinner of the English-Speaking Union; the day after that finds you going down the bay in the cutter to get a special interview with three members of the House of Representatives who have been investigating the PX's in the Western Zone of Germany. The next day, if it's March 17th and your name is O'Hara, Tom or John, but especially Tom, you go out in the rain or the cold, or both, and witness the annual Celtic defiance of pneumococci.

You go back to the office and try to write a dignified piece, without any phony begorra stuff, but getting in a few authentic touches for the benefit of these millions of Irish readers of the *Trib* who, as you can well imagine, will be lining up at the Cos Cob station to buy extra copies of the paper because of the cute picture of Deirdre Saltonstall, Maureen Griswold, and Desmond Codman, who were all down from Dorchester for the day and registering their sweet protests against Partition.

Brother Tom was given that assignment so often that we began to fear for him: every year, along about the first week in March, he would go into a brown study, which was appropriate enough since he is a Brown man, but his mood, we were well aware, had nothing to do with Brunonian loyalties. It was just that annual parade assignment hanging over him, a greenish cloud, so to speak. At long last the paper put him on politics, where he does very well indeed, thank you.

It might be argued that in New York politics, state and city, Republican and Democratic, every day's St. Patrick's Day, but that is not quite the case. Nowadays in a Tammany clubhouse the picture of Our Leader is just as likely to be that of a Forelli, a Goldberg, or an Evans as it is a Kelly, and in up-state Republican New York there is a Wadsworth for every Curran. The heeler, or as he would be called in modern terminology, the Statesman-on-the-Ward-Level, is not inevitably an Irishman. Consequently we are now completely free of graft and corruption, good government prevails everywhere, purity is the shibboleth, and I am Salmon P. Chase.

I never had the job of covering a St. Patrick's Day parade. I was either loaded or on night rewrite in those days. As a matter of fact I usually make a point of avoiding other Irishmen on the 17th. I wear me tie (this year I better: me boss brought me one from Ireland), I have been known to carry the blackthorn, and I have lifted me voice in praise of great and glorious St. Patrick (pray for that dear country, the country of our fathers) but where I go is to places that I am reasonably confident will be visited by a minimum of Irishmen, such as Tim Costello's. There I am safe. Nor Shaw, nor Yeats, nor Joyce will be there; only me. And for that night, if that night only, I am treated with respect by the hordes from Young Rubicam and Dancer-Fitzgerald-Sample-Donner & Blitzen, and their womenfolk. John Steinbeck has almost as much Irish blood as I have; moreover he talks with a shy little brogue, and he may be sitting in a booth at Tim's that night, but it's me they will listen to. There may and probably will be many among the hucksters who know a great deal more about Shaw, Yeats and Joyce than I ever will know, but they are on their best behavoir, celebrating Paddy's Day. And I represent part of the trappings, like the Jameson's whiskey they are drinking. Incidentally, I am forty-nine years old, my father's name was Patrick Henry O'Hara, his mother being a Franey; my mother is Katharine Delaney O'Hara, her mother being a Rourke, and I never yet have referred to the occasion as Paddy's Day. If that means I owe somebody an apology, I'd rather, as we used to say, owe it to you than stick you.

There are so many Irishisms that I am not acquainted with that I suppose I ought to be grateful to the Foreign Legion of the Men of Mayo for setting me straight. A relation-by-marriage by the name of Potter can always fill me in if I need filling in on the terrible goings-on at the Post Office whenever it was. And as to Irish literature, why, man, it took a Yale professor of Scandinavian origin to inform me that Will Shaxpere wrote in brogue. If I'd known that thirty years ago I might have been a different

man today. I'd have read less in Frank Sullivan and
Fitzgerald (not the Dancer partner mentioned above)
and more of Henry IV, Part I, which I am being ex-
posed to within hours of this writing.

One thing I have learned in all these years of appearing in public—appearing in print in public, I
mean—and that is, when you write about the Irish,
anything or anyone Irish, you had better be careful
what you say. Sometimes you almost wish you
hadn't said anything, and at other times you wish
you had become an apiarist. (For the benefit of certain of my Irish clientele, an apiarist is not a religious fanatic.) An Irish by-line, like mine, is all that
some fellows need as an excuse to write you letters
that apparently are intended to make you sign a confession and hang yourself. I do not by any means intend to imply that my fellow Irish are the only ones
who have found me guilty of kidnapping Charley
Ross and setting off the Black Tom explosion, but today I am in an advance St. Patrick's Day mood and
I am devoting myself to my own kind. No non-Irish
need apply. If you happen to be H. L. Crosby, or
John McCormack, or even Fiske O'Hara, singers all,
they'll die for you. But Theodore O'Hara, who wrote
"The Bivouac of the Dead" and Geoffrey O'Hara,
who wrote "K-K-K-Katy," and Kane O'Hara, the
playwright, who died June 17, 1782, must have got
the "Who do you think you are?" kind of mail that
often comes to this desk. However, I'm not com-

plaining. It may be good for Ted and Geoff and old Kane and young John to have such alert readers. For one thing, you must decide early on whether to be awfully careful what you say, or to say what you damn well please. Always, of course, with half an eye toward the beekeeping industry.

And it's people like some of the letter-writers who brought a little sunshine into my life this week. Apparently this Tex McCrary, broadcasting from the Waldorf-Astoria, likened the Porto Rican pistoleers to the Sinn Feiners of old, and boy, did he get slapped down! I didn't hear the original broadcast but I did catch him the next night, when he had Paul O'Dwyer to try to get him off the hook. McCrary may still be on the shambles, and it couldn't happen to a—well, now, I mustn't go Irish on you all of a sudden.

12.

Several years ago I got the call to speak at the Elizabethan Club of Yale University, Yale Station, Connecticut, which reminds me that in literary-scholastic circles I am what you might dub a club fighter. In the world of sport a club fighter is a young hopeful who can put on a good enough show for neighborhood fight fans, but isn't, and never will be, scheduled to throw punches at the Garden. That's me. I have spoken at The Lantern, Phillips Exeter; the Pipe & Quill, Lawrenceville; The English Club, Rutgers, and the Lizzie Club, Yale. But when it comes to the Big Time, in June, I am sitting on the beach at Quogue, Long Island, without a care in the world, or, at any rate, without having to worry about whether my tassel is hanging on the correct side of my mortarboard. I am an honorary member Psi Upsilon (Iota of Ohio chapter); an honorary member of the Princeton *Tiger* staff and of the Princeton University Right Wing Club, complete with watch charm and necktie pin, but after my name I can't even put Jr.

There was a time when I thought I was a shoo-in for at least an honorary master's (Master of Arts, not of foxhounds) at New Haven. I had always spoken well of the place and of most of its alumni. When the library asked me for some manuscripts for its American Collection, I forked over gladly. In fact, now I think of it, I am a Friend of the Yale Library. If the Yale Library ever needs any "O" type blood, I'm ready with a pint. If they're ever up a tree, call on me. If they're ever in a jam, here I am. As Cole Porter ('13 Ac.) has said, when other friendships are soon forgot, ours will still be hot.

What is more, Whit Griswold is an old friend of mine by virtue of the fact that we once courted first cousins, and when I was guest of honor at a party after my Lizzie Club talk, and the host asked me whom I wanted to see and I said Whit Griswold, my host didn't even know him. I said: "You better, because some day he's going to be president of this place." But for all the good Griswold did me in getting an honorary degree, I might as well have invited Arthur Twining Hadley.

Well the years came and went, and every June I would laugh at the not quite screamingly funny citations that go with honorary degrees, but I must admit there was a certain bitterness in my laughter; just a touch of frustration and envy, perhaps. I am, I think, all boy, and yet I began to understand how a town girl feels: I was all right to play around with during the school year, but at Commencement the Yale Fellows always had a date with Thurber, who probably never even heard of Gundlefinger, and wouldn't know Longley's from Langrock's. A man— or a town girl—can take only just so much of that kind of treatment, and no more. If Yale wants me, it knows where to reach me, but it better be nice or it'll get stuck with Mickey Spillane.

I have had much the same experience with a secret society called the National Institute of Arts and Letters. I am usually up in these matters, but the first I ever knew of the existence of the National Institute was through Marc Connelly. I had noticed that he always wore a little boutonniere, with tweeds or with evening clothes, and I asked him one night what it was. "The Legion of Honor?" I said, for I am color-blind. No, it wasn't the Legion of Honor, and he explained what it was in a way that clearly indicated that it was nothing I'd ever have to worry about.

I didn't worry about it either, until a friend of mine told me he had put me up and that I'd been voted down. I think I have been put up eight times, maybe more, and always have been given the cough drop. I'm not supposed to know this, but I have been put up by Philip Barry, Deems Taylor, Chauncey Brewster Tinker, Struthers Burt, William McFee and Louis Untermeyer, among others, all without consulting me, all out of the kindness of their hearts.

Indeed, Untermeyer once announced that he was going to get up and read all of my published works backwards until they elected me. That may have been a tactical error. There are some members of the Institute who would think my stuff reads better that way, and they don't want me to sound good.

The Institute is an organization that I still don't know much about. It has quasi-official status, in that it is chartered by the Congress of the United States. The members are chosen in much the same way that a form player picks horses: they go by performance in order to decide who among American writers have lasting, or staying, qualities. On that basis I probably qualify, since two of my gems, not just one, had early foot and are still legging it quite well after twenty years and fourteen years, with no immediate signs of tiring. I cannot, of course, say the same for anything at all that was written by some of the boys and girls who are in the Institute. But there probably are qualifications that I don't know about. One of the members, trying to console me, said not to feel badly, that it was just another line in *Who's Who*.

However, it's more than that. It's a big free dinner, and it is also a little something to wear in your lapel. I am just enough of a snob to like to have a little something in my lapel that will make other color-blind men think I belong to the Legion of Honor. I can't go around wearing my Right Wing wing or my Psi U badge. I don't own a Psi U badge. And in the Summer I can't wear my *Tiger* watch charm or even my Donaldson Award key, which looks like a Phi Beta Kappa key but is rarer, since there are only, I think, nine Donaldson keys and there are more than 100,000 Phi Betes.

Ernest Hemingway set a tempting precedent when he turned down the Institute some years ago, but he has all sorts of ribbons and boutonnieres. If it's good enough for John Steinbeck, it's good enough for me.

I am in a spot in relation to the Institute. It would be easy enough to knock it, to say that it's a group of mid-Victorians who couldn't possibly appreciate my work. The only trouble with that is—well, figure the ages of the men who have tried to get me in. The average would be, at a rough guess, close to seventy. I probably have been given the cough drop by people my own age, or younger. Naturally I score myself a better writer than most of the members, and the inferior of none. But that, to be sure, is only one man's opinion.

The only real consolation is that I am slightly worried about honors for writers. Without going to the trouble of making lists and walking across the room to check my theory, I suspect that election to the Academy (the inner circle of the Institute), and the Pulitzer Prize (for which I understand I was considered twice), and the movie Oscar (for which a script of mine was nominated), and all such bounties are not good for authors. Some enterprising youth might do a term paper on what happens to authors after they get honored all over the place. I have my misgivings (Miss Givings, take a letter).

13.

It's not the first time that has happened. What has happened? That I have begun a Sunday message with every intention of preaching on one topic, and almost immediately get diverted to something else. Heaven knows I am not at a loss for things to write about. Due to the tolerance of my boss—and a rather shabby trick I played in getting him to agree that I could write about authors, which means everybody— I'll never run out of things to say. My first aim is to entertain myself, thereby presumably entertaining you. So I do what I did last Sunday and other Sundays too: I begin by telling you that I once spoke at

the Elizabethan Club at Yale; from there I had intended to proceed with a discussion of my E Club
speech, but I wandered off and talked about other
matters.

I think I ought to go back to my E Club topic,
because it's important. Oh, it isn't important if you
spend your waking hours in a foolish effort to trisect
the angle, or are fascinated by the fact that the
reserves for rebuilding furnaces, etc., of Libbey-
Owens-Ford amounted last year to $3,576,880.46
(that's as of December 31, 1953; the picture may
have changed since then). If your idea of fun or a
life work is dressage, or calendar reform, or the romantic aspects of the rhododendron, or the calcula-
tion of time allowances in small-boat racing, you got
the wrong man. But you haven't got the wrong man
if you care anything about The Rewards of Writing,
which was my Yale topic.

Since I was expecting to address a gaggle of undergraduates, I wrote my little screed for the instruction of such as might be planning to make writing a
career. The meeting, I may say, was attended by
some of the oldest undergraduates I've ever laid
eyes on. As you know if you know old drinking
songs, there is always a hell of a situation up at Yale
(by the way, that "up" would seem to indicate that
the song was written by a Princeton man), and there
are always some juniors and seniors who quite
rightly are worried about their hairline; but mus-

taches! Well, of course what had occurred was that faculty and alumni, those who wanted to write and had not been hired by Harry Luce, had crashed the party. The academicians were taking a more than academic interest in writing's rewards.

And what are they?

Well, the tangibles. To get paid for something you like to do may take you out of the amateur class if you are a golfer or a tennis player or a jockey. You have to enter the clubhouse by a side door and you are not Mr. Steeplechaser, just J. Steeplechaser. But there is hardly any such thing as a good amateur writer. The playing of baseball, the throwing of punches, and the turning of phrases are three occupations that are best represented by the professional practitioners. I once spent part of an afternoon reading a history of the Schermerhorn family, but I have to admit that I spent the rest of the afternoon playing lawn tennis on the Schermerhorn lawn-tennis court. The tennis and the chronicles were in the amateur class, of interest, really, only to another Schermerhorn. I have seen one or two amateur efforts to make history of big-game hunting expeditions in Africa, and I have handled numerous volumes of the family-memorial type, such as war diaries and collected letters. They have their special value, but usually so very special that they are consulted only when somebody wants to prove that Great-grandpappy was at Chapultepec with Stonewall Jackson, or that a great-aunt had tea with Disraeli. And precisely because the books were written by amateurs we get nothing of what Disraeli said or how Jackson behaved. Practically all of these books have been privately printed, and for good reason. Occasionally you come across one that appeared in part in the old *Atlantic*, but Mr. Sedgwick paid off in silver cigarette boxes, like Piping Rock, and there was no necessity of reporting the author to the Authors League.

In another class we have the novels and volumes of verse that are arranged for by those firms so aptly called "vanity" publishers. They don't pay you, you pay them. That's about as amateur as you can get, practically on a par with building a defender of the America's Cup.

And yet all those publications were, to make the tired word more tired, rewarding. Holding the book in the hand, looking at the words in print—those experiences are the reward. Always, by the way, compared to the young mother's feelings on first looking at her newborn child. I don't know about that. I can tell you that holding my child for the first time was nothing like holding any book, so I am inclined to distrust that metaphor as I do all metaphors. However, the job well done, or done to the best of your ability, is a source of satisfaction that the amateur has in common with the professional.

I have always said that if I couldn't make my liv-

ing by writing, I'd get into another line. Starving
for one's art is my idea of nothing to do. When
friends have reminded me that I did on occasion go
on compulsory rations, I have had to reply that I
was no more starving for my art than an unemployed
subway guard is skipping the scoff for his particular
professional principles. Moreover, I wouldn't have
been starving if I could have got a job as a subway
guard. I was perfectly willing to push people into the
New Lots express if I could do so on a full stomach no
matter how heavy my heart might have been. I have
always wanted to be a writer, but an eating writer.

You can be a good writer and still make $25,000 a
year, or to put it in a subtly different way, you can
make $80,000 a year and still be a good writer.

If you bring up Dylan Thomas and his tragic pen-
niless death, I will remind you that T. S. Eliot has
a job, a job that he works at and for years has earned
his living at, and I will also remind you that our best
authors make money. I honestly do not believe that
there is today a fifty-two-year-old starving author
who can write as well as John Steinbeck, who eats
at 21. Ernest Hemingway can afford a magnum,
whether he buys it in a saloon or a gunsmith's, and
you're not going to tell me that there's a fifty-four-
year-old English teacher in Brown County, Indiana,
that can write rings around E. H. All I'll concede is
the possibility that there is someone who will be as
good as Hemingway and who now is twenty-five,

which is what Hemingway was when he published *In Our Time.*

The other reward is honours, a subject I more or less took care of last Sunday. And by the way, I hope you are not saving these pieces. You see, they are coming out in a book next year, and I want you to buy the book. End of commercial.

14.

Now that I've got on the general subject of the rewards of writing, I think I'll stay on it long enough to make a few remarks about the by-products of a writing career. The by-products in many cases are so diverting that it is only with great difficulty that some writers can remember where they started from, and consequently have trouble getting back to the main business.

I never have known a really first-rate writer who had that trouble, but in our country we have had some writers who were not quite really first-rate, who nevertheless have been important figures in

American writing. They are certainly worthy of our consideration in any discussion of American writers and writing, and they are most certainly worthy of consideration in this piece. Otherwise I'd have no point to make and while I am no slave to the art of making points, it is nice to make one now and then to keep one's hand in. You never know when you're going to have to make a point and if you lose your touch you lose your audience to somebody who wants to get back to McCarthy.

The by-products of the writing career are many, so many that instead of listing them in one attempt at all-inclusiveness, I'll just deal with them as they occur to me. The temptations of the by-products usually, but not always, follow soon after a writer's first major success. I say not always because the temptations sometimes are offered after the inno-cent writer has had a succession of failures. How-ever, it's usually after his first success, for obvious reasons. One of the first temptations is the opportu-nity to go out in Society.

Society, I have it on the word of people who don't know anything about it, no longer exists in this country. The disappearance of the stately homes of Newport, the razing of the Fifth Avenue town houses, and the popularity of the rather more simple life than that of forty years ago have been taken as proof that Society itself went bye-bye. The truth of the matter is that it is slightly more difficult for the

outsider to identify Society, but Society is, if anything, more there than ever.

It is now possible for a family to be very, very Society without having to build a ten-foot wall to advertise the fact. The Society people nowadays may
prefer to live in a house that's smaller than the porter's lodge on Grandfather's estate, but the smaller
house is if anything harder to get invited to.

For one thing, the modern Society people have
the legitimate excuse that they haven't room for anybody but their friends. Grandpa, with forty bed-
rooms in his Rhode Island cottage, would have
had room for the Republican National Convention.
Grandpa's grandson honestly couldn't offer accom-
modations to all the fellows in his group at Porcellian.

If you think that makes for a less exclusive Society
you haven't been following me. But to make it
tough, I shall now appear to contradict myself by
declaring that in modern Society an author who was
not born social has a better chance of observing the
upper crust than he would have in Grandpa's day. I
am not going to say that he has a better chance of
getting in and staying in, but any writer who makes
a good score, who observes ordinary rules of cleanli-
ness and politeness, and doesn't dress like a Texan or
a Broadway sharpie, will get invited to some Society
homes. He will not be asked to be godfather to the
Society children, he will not be tapped for the best

clubs, and there will be other more or less subtle ways of letting him know how far he can go, how much a part of Society life he can become, but if he is a good writer he will know what to expect, how much and how little, because in order to have made that good score professionally he will have had to be a sensitive man in the first place. The authors who have trouble and for whom the Society kick is a swift one in the pants are the ones who were not subtle enough, not sensitive enough.

I guess I know as much about Society as any author today. That statement may be momentarily misleading. I am not in Society; I'm not even in the *Social Register*, although I was a Dilatory Domicile for one issue, just for the record. But I have quite a few friends in Society, people I like a great deal because they are considerate, well-mannered, kind, undemanding and have their own private hells. The good ones are not overly suspicious, and for a writer to deprive himself of Society's society because, well for any reason, is a mistake, a professional mistake.

The money makes a difference between Society people and the rest of us, but it should not make the big difference to a writer. At least the money and family backgrounds shouldn't make the difference that it does for most writers who force themselves to be fascinated by, let us say, sharecroppers, when in background these writers are just as far removed from the sharecroppers' way of life as they are from the Reading Room at Newport. I know the rich, and I am not going to be told by any graduate of the University of Wisconsin that he knows more than I do about the poor.

A writer should be able to take this by-product called Society—and to leave it alone, leave it be. It isn't difficult, given proper balance to start with. For a year, including two summers of the deceptively simple life, a writer can have a better time, just the physical comforts, than he would have by getting in the way at some hardscrabble farm. The Society rich, as so often has been said, know how to live. They are accomplished hands at getting the most out of their money. I'd much rather stay at the Waldorf than at some fleabag in West Madison Street, Chicago, and I am sure of that because I've stayed at both. I am now staying at neither. I am living at a place, and on a scale, that I can manage. If I had some professional project that required my bedding down again on Skid Row I'd go, but when I'd finished my work I'd get out. I would be a phony to stay, giving my blood to the seam-squirrels when I didn't have to. I would be just as big a phony if I refused to see likeable Society people because they happened to have been born that way.

It has been my experience of Society that an author starts with some entertainment value, even if he doesn't open his yap. You go to a Society party and there, as any place else, you meet the world's two major classes: those who have read you, and those who have not. There is another classification, and that is the people who regard an author as a freak, but you will soon find out that they are not securely Society. They are still in that tentative phase where they think it is part of the Society act to regard authors as freaks. The real thing among Society people regard only freaks as freaks. It's worth bearing in mind. Keeps you from wasting your time with the semi-mains.

Between this writing and my next appearance I will have renewed acquaintance with still another form of life, which I have not investigated in seven years. You must have guessed that I refer to Hollywood. That's another by-product of authorship, and it always amused me to hear a writer knocking Society and then admitting that the night before he had spent six hours at the home of a movie producer.

15.

If this dispatch should turn out to have a strange, if not exactly exotic, sound as though it had been written in a foreign land, it will be because I have not been able to conceal the fact that I am writing from Los Angeles, California.

As some of my more alert and devoted customers are aware, I have been keeping myself quite busy latterly. It is better to keep busy, and I am for the moment not speaking exclusively of the moola department when I say it is better to keep busy. Better for an author, better for regular people—I have two jobs, of which this is one. The other (which is no secret from my local bosses, who themselves are extremely well-read and hip guys) finds me in the pulpit on a fortnightly basis, guiding and instructing four million readers through the intricacies and subtleties of the entertainment world. For my larger audience (which, though larger, gets me only twice a month instead of every Sunday) I must occasionally leave my fireside for little or big trips, and that's why I am in Los Angeles now, and homesick.

But as I say, it is better to keep busy.

I have given considerable thought to the subject of idleness. I guess we all have, and I'm afraid I have come reluctantly to the conclusion that idleness is un-American. I am supported in this conclusion by none other than the late George Bernard Shaw, a man who didn't have mere opinions; he handed out dogma. Some years ago a friend of mine named Irving Netcher, who died last year, was, as was his custom, sunning himself at the right season for sunning oneself on the French Riviera. He was delighted, one day, to be invited to call on Shaw, whom he had seen but had not met. After the how-do-you-do's Shaw said something like this: "Mr. Netcher, you probably are wondering why I invited you to tea. Well, I invited you to tea because I wanted to inspect the only American I've ever seen who could be idle gracefully."

Irving Netcher was a charming man whose family had made their money in a Chicago department

store. Irving went to Yale, where I believe he was
Phi Beta Kappa without making that his career, and
after doing his war chore in 1918 he settled down, if
that's quite the phrase, to what might be called a
frenetic loaf. He married Rosie, one of the fabulous
Dolly Sisters, and Irving and Rose, I think I am
safe in saying, became as well loved as any American couple I've ever known. It was always a pleasure
to encounter them in 21 or at New York parties.

One summer they took a house in Westhampton
not far from mine in Quogue and I suppose the tax
on their liquor bills just about covered the expense
of the nearby Coast Guard station. They spent most
of their time on the Riviera and in Palm Springs,
California, the while maintaining a flat in New
York for in-between visits. They lived in Tahiti,
London, Paris, Palm Beach, and when I say lived I
mean lived it up. At least once to my knowledge
Irving put a Cadillac aboard a freight airplane and
had it sent to France, and was able to convince me
that in so doing he was saving money.

But there are few Irving Netchers. I am slightly
acquainted with a multimillionare who does things
on an even grander scale than Irving did. This second spender gives the big party and charters the big
yacht, and offers the Windsors as bait, but I cannot
call him a successful idler. Neither he nor his missus
seems to have as much fun as the Netchers had, and
I know they never inspired any affection. This man,

it happens, is named Charlie, but Good-Time—no.
I have another friend, a man my own age, who is
impressively rich and who lived it up all his life,
renting Venetian palaces and hiring the orchestra
to come back to his hotel after the ball was over—
but my contemporary was a bit of a cheat. He was
a secret worker. When everybody else was sleeping
it off, my friend was on the telephone to his office
or his broker, and instead of blowing his partly in-
herited stack, he has made so much money that he
can afford to go around the world first-class and take
a couple of people as his guests, which he is doing
as I write. Secret workers are disqualified, even
though they might plead that they have fun with
their venture capital. In the American language
loafer is such a strong term of opprobrium—unless
you're talking about shoes—that I hesitate to apply
it to a friend, and the word idler conjures up a
Beerbohm caricature of a man with a foot-long cigarette holder and a suspiciously epicene manner.

And so the authors. The late, great Percy Ham-
mond once offered as his definition of fun: "Not
writing." Well, Percy was a fascinating stylist who
operated in the theater, and to him writing a review was practically torture. I used to watch him
after he came back from the play. He would disrobe
down to his silken shirt and tailored trousers (but
usually keeping on his velour hat), send a copy boy
out for a half-pint of gin, and begin to fight the

deadline. In his last years the review became shorter
and shorter and had to be leaded out so much that
there was about four times as much white space in
his piece as there is between the lines of the chronicle you are reading. But Percy was not an author
and neither, really, was F. P. A., another writer who
hates writing. F. P. A. was a paragrapher, an editor,
and a composer of excellent light verse, but I can't
give him his author's badge. Heywood Broun used to
write a piece about the things an author does in an
effort to get down to work, but it was part of his
act. Broun was a natural-born writer. Twenty minutes was all he needed to do one of those *World*
columns and there never has been anything like
them.

Of course it's understandable that authors can
hate work, the work that they love and live by.
There must be five or ten million men and women
in this country who are earning their living at work
that they enjoy, that they picked in their teens and
have been engaged in ever since. Among those millions are, I am pretty sure, all newspaper men and
women (editorial side, of course), all doctors, most
lawyers, architects, locomotive engineers, painters,
actors and actresses (although a pitifully large number of actresses have Mother to blame), ball players,
college professors, steeplejacks, sailors in submarines,
airline pilots, snake charmers, clergymen, mathema-
ticians, masseurs, poolroom house men, musicians,

telephone linemen and forest rangers, to name a few occupations that involve pleasurable activity and special skill. Men and women so occupied love their work, but at the same time they often grouse about it, squawk about the hours, look forward to vacation, and do an almost convincing imitation of victims of slavery. In a triumphant restatement of the obvious I call your attention to the fact that you can love your work and hate it in much the same way, to the same degree, that you can love a woman and still have moments of feeling like belting her one for luck. Mind, now, I am not recommending this disorderly procedure. I'm just calling attention to it.

With writers this is approximately how it works: you finish a novel or a play, and you are entitled to your vacation. If all goes financially well, you may yield to the temptation to stretch the vacation beyond a healthy spell. The unhealthy spell begins at the precise moment that you begin to make excuses for not returning to work. And if those excuses seem enormously valid, you better look out, for that's the first sign that you are losing to idleness. However, I have found it true in my own case and with author friends of mine that the hidden desire to get back to work is revealed when you start to write long, unnecessary letters. One of these Sundays I shall write about inter-author correspondence.

16.

Wolcott Gibbs is going to ruin his eyes.

I am in a position to make that doleful prediction because I happen to be using his typewriter, and as the compositor who is setting up these lines will tell you, the ribbon on the Gibbs typewriter is strictly Confederate—a defeated gray line. Unlike the author who grips your attention for the moment, Gibbs is near-sighted. What the world looks like to a near-sighted man is something your far-sighted visionary can only imagine, but even with my spectacles on I am having trouble. The typing has that distant appearance, like the bottom page of a mimeographed menu in a cheap restaurant. You know: Y-nk-e P-t R-ast, GF cents. If you have less than GF cents in your pocket you are in trouble. Settle for a ham on rye and avoid arguments.

Some playwrights—and since I pay dues to the Dramatists Guild I may properly call myself a playwright—would have a field day with the circumstances that Critic Gibbs is near-sighted and uses inkless ribbons in his typewriter. Having been treated fairly by Critic Gibbs, I have no complaints against his reviews. Moreover, he disliked *Tea and Sympathy* almost as much as I did, which is evidence that wisdom and taste are not possessed solely by us far-sighted ones.

I had lunch with Gibbs today. Both of us are on the wagon, so the conversation was animated, brilliant, and as might be expected of two men who have known each other for twenty-six years, classified material. I may say, however, that following our custom, we re-examined certain human frailties, such as the nocturnal, the fiscal and so on. After one of these lunches a kind of euphoria takes hold—at least in my case—because in all the world there are are only two men who are so free of pomposity, gallant but not silly in their relations with the opposite sex, gifted writers but not competitors, figures of consequence in Upper Middle Bohemia, men of experience without being dwellers in the past, and friends of Abner Drury. Abner Drury was a prep-school roommate of mine. We are also friends of Allan Cullum. Allan Cullum went to prep school with Gibbs. Gibbs knew Drury and I grew up with Cullum and those facts were enough for Gibbs and enough for me in 1928, for to have been a friend of Drury's and Cullum's meant that you led a certain kind of life, and if you have been following these essays closely, you'll know what kind of life I mean. For detail let me just say that Holy Orders never was seriously contemplated by any of the four of us, once we got going. Gibbs never knew Chink Youngfleisch, but I'm sure they'd have been friends.

We kicked it around so much at lunch that I forgot about the clipping from *The New York Times* that I had in my pocket. If I had remembered I'd have turned it over to Gibbs for his opinion and, possibly, obtained a quote for you. Gibbs is under contract to the *New Yorker*, but I would have risked a law suit. That Other *Times,* as we sometimes refer to it on these premises, has a department, unsigned, called "Topics of the Times" on its editorial page, wherein they act frivolous. *New York Times*-frivolous, that is. You are in no danger of a ruptured appendix from any belly-laughs the 43rd Street crowd might give you.

Somewhat rashly our New York neighbor has decided that a safe subject for some gentle joshing is the photographs of authors on the dust jackets of their books. I quote: "Certain aspects of the passing show are characterized by the fact that they never have to change. Variety in this category is anathema. Not to be mysterious about these certain aspects, here is a sampling. Pre-season baseball-camp photographs. Opening night at the opera. Models being named Miss Wood Pulp Industry. Lost little boys shown wearing policemen's hats and licking ice cream cones. And finally, at least for the purposes of this discussion, photographs of authors on the dust jackets of their books. These pictures usually depict the author doing one of two things. Either he is staring from under intelligent brows, dramatically lighted, a cigarette dangling dreamily from his lips, or he is shown in profile, seated at his typewriter. In this kind of picture the author's hair is neatly combed, he is freshly shaved, his shirt (sleeves rolled up, collar open, no tie) looks fresh and unwrinkled and his desk is a model of neatness. If we could see the floor in this picture, it would undoubtedly be as neat as the author."

As steady customers of this stand know, I have been conducting studies of auctorial habits since December, and I am somewhat dismayed to discover *The New York Times* tickler of funnybones poaching on my territory. Not that I claim any exclusive right. It isn't that that dismays me. What grieves me is that *The New York Times*, upon which thousands of readers rely for information, can so seriously misinform. For they were obviously writing about a photograph of me on one of my dust jackets, showing me in semi-profile at my typewriter. The picture appeared in *The New York Times* some years back.

My hair was slicked down and I was freshly shaved and my shirt was fresh and unwrinkled. I stared from under intelligent brows, dramatically lighted (that had me for a minute, but what they mean is that I was lighted dramatically), but then began the bad reporting. The cigarette, which I thought was dramatically lighted, did not dangle dreamily from my lips, or from my nose, or from my ears. It was in my hand. My cuffs were buttoned, I was wearing a small-figure necktie and my collar was closed. The floor was as neat as the author. In my house you are not confined to the kitchen floor; you can eat off the living-room floor, bedroom floor, study floor, hall floor, laundry floor, or bathroom floor. We are very strict about that, because true hospitality demands that a guest may eat off any floor he chooses, and at the same time I don't like my guests getting in Thelma's way. It's all right if they want to crowd into Thelma's kitchen when she has gone for the night, but I expect my visitors to be ladies and gentlemen and I keep my other floors neat for that very reason.

And what ruffian would pose for a *New York Times* photograph with his collar open? As soon go to a Gridiron dinner in black tie.

17.

You have it on my authority that Louis Kronenberger is a man of taste and discrimination but
writes about the theater for Harry Luce, and has
been doing so since 1938. As one of his many pred-
ecessors in that job (lasting considerably less than
sixteen years) I've often wondered how he did it.
That is, how he could write those anonymous pieces
for so many years, handle the intra-office political
maneuverings that are always going on at 9 Rocke-
feller Plaza, keep a firm hold on a job that every
second undergraduate in the United States thinks
he could do better—and keep an equally firm grip

on his sanity. Well, that's a rhetorical wondering. I know how Louis does it. The *Time* job provides the base pay, as did Samuel Pepys' Navy post, as did Dr. Watson's medical practice, as Gipsy Rose Lee's public unveilings were, you might say, a cover for her authorship of novels, with the difference, to be sure, that Kronenberger's *Time* work is anonymous and his non-*Time* work is more revealing and signed.

Kronenberger is always busy away from the steady job. He can teach you lessons in Henry Mencken and Henry Adams, if you happen to be going to Brandeis University. He is to the Theater Arts what Benny Friedman is to football. His book *Kings and Desperate Men* is a widely admired work on life in eighteenth-century England, his novel *Grand Right and Left* is a pretty funny satire on the richest man in the world, and he has acted as editor and anthologist of more collections than W. W. Jacobs has appeared in. (I just counted up.) Kronenberger is a highbrow, but he is a kind of highbrow that I like.

You go to Louis and Emmy Kronenberger's for dinner and you have a good time. The scoff is good, the booze flows like booze; if you've just been saying that you haven't seen Archie MacLeish in six years, you'll probably see Archie MacLeish; or Lillian Hellman, or Irwin Edman, or Cassie and John (Mason) Brown. If you are living in New York and go to the

Kronenbergers' you get that sense, so rare in New York, that you are visiting in a home. The presence of young children has something to do with it, but not everything. I've been to hundreds of New York apartments that housed anywhere from one to six children, and in all financial grades, without getting that home feeling. The fact that you know the Kronenbergers' dinner parties are carefully planned has nothing to do with it either. . . . As a certain brilliant author once said in one of his brilliant plays: "Don't take it apart; you might not be able to put it together again."

You gather by this far down that the Kronenbergers are friends of mine. But have you been quick? Are you way ahead of me, you cute thing? Have you guessed that I'm going to say something about *Company Manners,* Louis' latest book? You dog, you. I love ya.

When I read the announcements of the book, which is subtitled "A Cultural Inquiry Into American Life," I knew that this was one I couldn't skip. I waited the conventional fortnight for my free copy, then I began wrestling with myself, Graeco-Roman rules, and stalked into Doubleday's Fifth Avenue shop and slapped the cash on the barrelhead. (This has nothing to do with the book under examination, but have you noticed that the young men in that Doubleday's apparently go home in the evening, put on turtleneck sweaters, and pick up a buck or two by exercising East Side dogs? What a well rounded existence! What a healthy life they lead! What fascinating stories they must tell! What do you hear from Noel?)

I carted the book home with me, when what I should have done was reserve a drawing room on the Century. As I have told you on some of our previous Sunday outings, I am highly susceptible to household distractions. I am only too willing to have a game of catch, take my beating at Pegity, and tell stories. The temptations are there all the time, and that's one reason why I should have grabbed the overnight rattler and devoted myself to the new Kronenberger, taking care first of all not to buy any newspapers or magazines. A train or a steamship always means reading to me, but especially now, in my delicate condition of temperance.

But I brought the book home and I have been fighting it ever since. You'd fight it too if you had in mind the publication of a book on manners, and discovered a good book already published. For instance, now, many years ago I invented a name for a type I don't like. I named him a John-caller, meaning simply a person who calls you John on the very first meeting. Kronenberger holds forth at quite some length on John-calling and he's right all the way. Then you may recall that a little while ago (but safely long enough ago to absolve me of suspicion of theft) I made a few sarcastic remarks about people who write and address you as "Dear John O'Hara," not "Dear Mr. O'Hara" or "Dear John." Hear Kronenberger on the subject: "All the more outrageous, because it is so trifling, is the whole business of first names. To go at it a little obliquely, there is—for one thing—the recent but already ubiquitous custom, among this new race, of addressing perfect strangers as 'Dear William Smith.' Temperamentally, I happen to find the custom loathsome because it even sounds ugly and unnatural. As a special kind of salutation it has, to be sure, a considerable history. Henry James might write to a very much younger man (because he knew the man's family and because, one might add, he was Henry James) 'Dear Mr. Arthur Benson,' and then drop the 'Mr.' before dropping the Benson; and on occasion, from having friends in common or a sort of equal public standing, people might address other people they had not met as 'Dear Harry Jones.' But this was a way of saying 'We aren't really strangers,' where the usage today is a forcible way of confessing we are; for, at the first meeting or by the second letter, these people shift to the straight-out use of first names. Many of them are not yet twenty-five years old. I very much doubt that they mean to be presumptuous; I very much imagine that they wish to be correct. And as this is the common coin of their elders and superiors, it seems right out of Emily Post."

Then, later: "If a man can call you by your first name, he has you at an unfair advantage. In the eyes of the world, he has some small claim on you which you, at the cost of seeming ungracious or even treacherous, may be forced to deny. First-naming may be a mere phase, of a piece with women in Jane Austen's time [And our own.— J. O'H.] addressing men by their last names, but the one strikes as false and familiar a note as the other."

You ought to get a hold of this book, with or without a roomette reservation. I recommend it. The fact that the Kronenbergers gave me a beautiful big George Washington desk which I work at every day has nothing to do with my recommendation. Any more than Louis' own ingratitude. He now says he hates gadgets, but there was a time when he liked them and I bought him an expensive Mark Cross gadget. If I hadn't had it stamped I'd demand its return, and he could come and get his desk.

18.

I was breaking the Sabbath stillness a few Sabbaths back with a few pop-offs about honours. Ah, pop-offs! Will you ever forget those wonderful Sunday mornings in the 16th Arondissement when you made those lovely pop-offs for breakfast? Only we called them fiacres. I wonder what ever became of Mimi, the midnight midinette. Probably ended up in a Gene Kelly picture.

But enough of these raffish recollections. I was, and am once again, speaking of honours, which I spell that way for a reason. The reason is that honours with the built-in "u" looks more impressive than without it. I never was a First in Greats at Cambridge, but I was valedictorian of my prep-school class, with top Honours in English and Spanish, and if I were to say I took top Honors you wouldn't be impressed at all, would you?

After the blaze of glory with which I terminated my prep-school career (and it had other spectacular aspects besides the aforementioned), I went four years without another honour. I was engaged in newspaper work, covering such items as mining disasters and church suppers, both of which were making their contributions to my eventual duodenal ulcer. If you cover a mining disaster, you don't feel like eating, and if you cover as many church suppers as I have, you don't feel like eating veal. Anyway, I did four years in the small-town newspaper business and then decided that New York and I were ready for each other. Through the good offices of F. P. A., my talents were given a temporary home by the *Herald Tribune*. In those days F. P. A.'s column, The Conning Tower, was appearing in the *World*, and it was an honour to get a contribution printed in it. But more of an honour was to get a mention in his weekly diary, and still more of an honour was to be mentioned in his Gotham Gleanings.

Well, folks, your boy made it. I can remember it now: "J. O'Hara, of Pottsville, Pa., has accepted a position on Ogden Reid's newspaper." If Joe Sayre

is to be believed, I must have been one of the fresh-
est squirts ever to hit the Type & Print Club. I wore
a coonskin coat, a bowler and carried a Malacca
stick. According to Sayre's version, I would appear on
a story and would use the cane as a teacher uses a
pointer, or a leftenant does a swagger stick. Or—this
is not Sayre's version, but what he implied—as a field
marshal uses a baton. There was nothing unusual
about carrying a cane in the late twenties. All the
young bloods at Dan Moriarty's 58th Street branch
of the Racquet Club carried canes, and all newspaper men, including the rating of copyboy. It was
not the cane itself, but the way I gestured with it,
according to Sayre, that made veteran reporters suspect that I was the boy Roy Howard. Then when
they learned the awful truth I was sat down hard.
Now I'm crowding fifty, but there are still a lot of
guys in the newspaper business who will not be de-
ceived by the new dignity or the growth of gray. At
least three newspaper men call me "Kid," and I'll bet
they'd be a little resentful if I called them "Dad."

The first night I went to work on the *Trib* I made
the acquaintance of Don Skene and Frank Sullivan.
Skene was covering prize fights for the *Trib*, and
Sullivan was writing columns for the *World* and the
Sunday World. Sometimes Frank ran The Conning
Tower when F. P. A. was away, sometimes he con-
ducted Heywood Broun's column, sometimes he
edited the *Blotz*, which was a parody newspaper

printed in the *Sunday World*. He and Skene were Big By-Line Men to me, and I felt important indeed on that first meeting when they spent a good part of the evening convincing me that I ought to call myself John O'Hara rather than John H. O'Hara.

When the *World* ended—and it did for many people in February 1931—Sullivan wrote oftener for the *New Yorker,* some of the funniest stuff the magazine has printed. Whenever he brings out a book of funny pieces the reviews knock themselves out trying to be just as funny, in the same manner, and their total failure is the best proof of how uniquely funny Sullivan can be. But let me wander back to the subject: Honours.

The *New Yorker* has a few traditions, such as reprinting the Optimist joke and running the beaver-hatted Beau New Yorker, or Eustace Tilley, on the cover every anniversary issue, or every anniversary issue they remember to, in the case of the Optimist joke. But those are more or less special, intramural traditions. The one that the public knows about is Frank Sullivan's Christmas greetings poem. I should know, but I don't, how Sullivan came to write the first of those poems. I'm not even sure of the date. . . .

May I interrupt myself?

I got so curious about the date of the first Sullivan Christmas card that I sent him the following telegram: PLEASE WIRE PREPAID AND NONE OF

THAT COLLECT STUFF THE DATE OF YOUR
FIRST CHRISTMAS GREETING. Then I knocked
off for a while awaiting his reply. I print his reply:
DID FIRST CHRISTMAS GREETING FOR NEW
YORK WORLD ABOUT 1929. DID ONE FOR
MAGAZINE JUDGE IN 1931 AND DID FIRST
ONE FOR THE NEW YORKER IN 1932. ESTI-
MATE I WILL RUN OUT OF NAMES ABOUT
1980. COLLIERS IS WONDERFULLY IM-
PROVED LATELY. WHAT CAN IT BE?

Well, there's a Sweet & Sour exclusive for you,
straight from the Feedbag of Saratoga Springs, Mr.
Frank Sullivan. I'm not sure of the exact date I first
appeared in the Greeting, and it's after 9 o'clock so
I wouldn't want to bother Sullivan with another telegram. I'd hate to disturb him. At nine o'clock he's
sure to be at the New Worden bar, incapable of
reading a telegram and with only the dimmest recollection of who I am. But I can tell you that getting
in his Christmas poem was a triumph. In later years
he has ignored me in favor of members of my family, but I can loftily say I made it in, I think, 1934.

I suppose I used to have a lot of crust, if Sayre's
picture is correct, but I never have been able to ask
Sullivan one question I've always wondered about:
"When, Sullivan, do people start being nice to you in
the hopes of getting in the Christmas Greeting?" A
great many people go to his home town in August to
study the thoroughbred horse. That gives those peo-

ple a certain advantage. I usually send him a telegram on his birthday, September 22nd, well after
getaway day, but that's as far as I'll go and I have
found that the man can't be bribed but I'll bet a lot
of people try.

Sullivan has a new book out called *Sullivan Bites
News,* subtitled "Perverse News Items," with pictures
by Sam Berman. It has a laugh every other page,
and before you start accusing me of being ungener-
ous to a friend, buy the book and find out that it's
only on every other page that there is text and picture. If you are acquainted with Sullivan humor you
will be delighted to know that this book is a sort of
advanced-degree course in his study of the American cliché, in this instance the newspaper cliché,
particularly the kind of thing that we still put in
one-column boxes. What we really ought to do with
most of them is put them in leaden boxes, like Navy
codebooks, and drop them over the side.

I haven't seen Sullivan in a long time, too long. He
seems to have settled like cement in Saratoga. I have
one thought to offer. It has always been my theory
that it finally will be an Irishman who will put Mc-
Carthy in his place. An Irishman not too far removed from these pages is working on the project, in
a serious vein. In a lighter vein the man to do it is
Sullivan.

19.

Frankly, friends, I was almost going to say a few words about Texas.

I came limping to my lectern without an idea in my head, a not unique situation, to be sure, but this time it was dangerous, and I will have to explain why.

You see, I am a professional writer, with strong and fairly numerous beliefs about what a professional writer should be able to do. One of my beliefs is that a pro should be able to write a piece today for a Sunday in November 1957, and another belief that with me is practically an article of faith is that the pro should be able to come so close to the deadline that the Confederates are taking a bead at you, and escape unscathed.

It's just about thirty years that I've been a pro, and in that time, I have missed not a single deadline. But for the past day or two I have been worried, I don't quite know why, for fear no idea would come along before the last hour that copy could be handed to the printer.

Last night I sat in the jolly company of a famous actor, a famous cartoonist and two handsome women. At about the moment that the slowest cabaret musician has put away his sarrusophone for the night, your obedient servant was sitting in an obscure crib, but his heart, or rather his conscience, was in Trenton.

"Do we look tight to you?" said the actor.

"Do I look sober to you?" said I, which was my cowardly or perhaps polite way of evading a comment on the condition of the cartoonist, who was manfully struggling with a rucksack that contained several Rob Roys, several beers, several Scotches, one stinger, and several more Scotches. The rucksack, of course, was on his back. In any event, there I was, looking like Old Sobersides, which indeed I am but I don't want to look it, and paying no attention to the wit and romance about me. Just worrying about what to say this week.

Well, here I am, the old pro, by golly. For not

only have I come up with an idea. I have come up
with an idea that is so new, so original, so clever and
everything, that before you read another word you
better go over to the work basket and get your scissors. You're going to want to clip this one out and
carry it around with you. If this doesn't make you
glad you're alive on May 2, 1954, you're just too
hard to please. You're in on a historic event.

I'll give it to you slowly.

In the last couple of weeks I've noticed some ads
and reviews about a book called *Country Store,* by
Gerald Somebody. I've been meaning to get the
book and maybe do a piece on it, but something
always kept me from getting it. I would be in a
hurry to catch a train, or I would be thinking of
something else when I was in the vicinity of a book-
shop, or, like last night, when the sarrusophone
player was packing up, I didn't feel it was the right
moment to ask the waiter or the cigarette girl for a
copy of a volume that I wasn't sure of the title of or
of the name of the author of.

However, I pride myself in being a fairly re-
sourceful man, and that's how you happen to be a
witness to literary history.

I am going to review a book that I know nothing
about, which has already been published, which I
feel I could have done better, and which I may
write some day. If you are even slightly confused,
may I remind you that that's often the way with

historic events. Don't forget that the Battle of New Orleans was fought after the war was over. Remember that Cornell-Dartmouth game with the extra down. And I remind you once again that Cornwallis didn't surrender at Yorktown.

Now the reason I know I would write a better *Country Store* than Gerald did is that Gerald never worked for my grandfather and never set foot in his store, and any book called *Country Store*, or *General Store*, would have to be about J. I. Delaney's store in Lykens, Dauphin County, Pa. I never heard of anybody named Gerald in Lykens. I knew a man named Wellington Voss, and another named Haridan Randall, and another named Bindley Hoff, but nobody named Gerald. (I had a classmate named Jerry Madden, from Toronto, and another classmate named Jerry Howard, from Brooklyn, but neither of them ever set foot in Lykens.)

I don't care how good Gerald's book is. He couldn't have known about Ambrose Bupp. There was a time around 1910, when I thought Ambrose Bupp was one of the greatest, and certainly one of the nicest, men in the world. Ambrose drove for my grandfather. (Whose name, by the way, was Joseph Israel Delaney, and he was the nicest man that ever lived, bar none.) In the mornings Ambrose filled the boxes with the groceries and stuff that the customers had ordered, and in the afternoons he delivered the boxes, and I was allowed to ride on the front seat with Ambrose, and take the reins going up steep hills. I was also permitted to take the brake off at the bottom of hills, and help put up the tailboard. I was forbidden to ride the step on the back of the wagon.

Every afternoon, as soon as the Pennsy passenger train departed for Harrisburg (Lykens was the end of the line on both Pennsy and Reading), we would start out on deliveries, but our first stop was not exactly a delivery. It was the Exchange Hotel, which had an iron watering trough. Grandpa always had a good, spirited team, but they would stand still at the Exchange Hotel while Ambrose went in to get a cigar. When I reached manhood I understood why Ambrose's cigars had an aroma that was different from those that my own father used to keep for Monsignor McGovern. I detected the same aroma last night on the cartoonist, and he was only smoking cigarettes.

Once in a while Ambrose would not show up for work, and his duties would be taken over by one of the Hoffman boys. When I asked my grandfather what was the matter with Ambrose, my grandfather would explain that Ambrose had his asthma again. Several times my grandfather fired Ambrose for getting asthma too often, but he always took him back when it got cured.

As a boy I met E. T. Stotesbury and Agnew T. Dice, and as a senior delinquent I have known some

Harrimans and Hills and other railroad names, but even trips on private cars (three) have not really impressed me as much as a freight car loaded with flour or a gondola lying on the spur in my grandfather's lumber yard. At that time I didn't know about demurrage, so I was disappointed when the car was unloaded and taken out of the yard. I believed—and for all practical purposes it was true—that my grandfather owned those cars and that I thus had the right to climb all over them, giving hand signals to a mythical crew, and supplying my own sound effects.

I suppose Gerald's book covers adequately the sights and smells of a small-town store; the barrel of dill pickles and the Gail & Ax and the beautifully made chests of Number 50 cotton and the Hecker's catalogue-almanacs and the brass tacks for measuring muslin and the Dietz lanterns and the dried figs and sugar cocoanut (that I used to pretend was Miner's Extra chewing tobacco). But Gerald never heard my grandfather tell a miner that Stiney now had enough money saved up so he could send to the Old Country for his woman. And I'll bet Gerald's store didn't have a wire doormat studded with marbles, and wooden pails filled with Keebler & Weyl's sweet cakes. And I know darn well he never saw the sights I saw when I delivered groceries on Polish Row.

20.

One of the funniest little jokies that never fails to bring tears of laughter to the eyes of publishers is the legend that authors don't care anything about money. "Don't care anything about money!" they will say. "Well, you just try and bargain with an author if you think they don't care about money."

They, the publishers, seem to think that we, the authors, are frauds when we hold out for all the money we can get and the best possible terms. They seem to believe that we are sinful hypocrites, devious and venal, sharp and sly. According to the universally held belief of publishers, an author is a chiseler who pretends to be high-minded about moola, but who gets his greatest pleasure in disappointing those poor, put-upon men who get their greatest pleasure in making authors famous. A portrait of a publisher by a publisher would be that of a gentleman of distinction whose waking hours were taken up by eleemosynary activity, directed mostly in the interests of writers.

Over the years, and not without some reason, the legend grew that authors are not businessmen. An author, according to the legend, is a commercial illiterate who doesn't know the difference between a bond and an acceptance. In the legend, an author barely knows the difference between Over the Counter and Under the Table. And, I cheerfully admit, the legend is based on fact. Most authors are financial flunkers. The only author friend of mine who knew his way around Wall Street was Philip Barry. There must be others, but they aren't friends of mine.

Very well. I concede the fact in the legend, and that's exactly the way the publishers would like it to be. Authors ought to take what they are offered, but unfortunately for the publishers, some authors remain on speaking terms with some other authors, and the word has got around that if you write a book you can get a 15 percent royalty, not just 10 percent. But if you haggle, if you try to get the best possible terms, you will hear howling and wailing; the publisher who likes to think of the author as a weirdie who resides on Cloud 85, just can't stand it, that's all.

It could, of course, make you wonder what kind of people publishers are. There seems to be no doubt that ideally an author would be a man who has learned his profession well enough to earn his living at it; to have lived and traveled and read and studied and observed, and put down on paper with some effectiveness as much of the living and observation as he wishes to communicate. He usually is a man who at some time or other has earned his living at something besides writing. He has worked hard, he has qualified. Sensitivity, alertness, active intelligence and work have made him a pro. Well, this man, with all those qualifications, is then supposed to hand over his work to a businessman and to accept in return the absolute minimum of money. He is not supposed to know anything about money, he is not supposed to care anything about money. If he does know something about money, if he does hold out for money, he is a nonconformist, an unartistic pretender. He becomes the object of the publishers' sarcasm while they remain knights in armor that would be shining if the writers would leave them enough money to buy polish. The only trouble with the knightly comparison is that it's totally inaccurate. A knight is supposed to be chivalrous; a publisher's ambition is to outsmart a man who hasn't learned decimals. A publishing house is not a home.

It is one of my theories about writing that everything an author does, everything, can be made useful. I had occasion recently *in loco parentis* to give some advice to a young man who wants to be a writer. He is just getting out of college, where he wrote a little, and he was crying the blues because he thought he had wasted time by not having tried for summer jobs that were connected with writing. I consoled him by showing him how valuable his non-writing jobs could be, how much more valuable, in fact, than poking away at a novel or short stories. But the next time I see him, I may suggest that he take a night course in accounting at NYU. He will meet some people he would not have met otherwise, and he will be ready to handle publishers when his time comes. I know I've often wished I were able to say, in the most offhand way, during a publisher luncheon: "I've been looking over that new contract, and I was just thinking I'd never seen anything like it in all the years I worked for Price, Waterhouse, and a pal of mine at Ernst & Ernst agreed with me." The bitter truth is that I am one of the legendary type authors. I own a pathetic little portfolio of securities and I couldn't even tell you what they are. You may be sure they do not affect the fact that I have to work for a living.

You have surmised that something happened that got me off on this economics kick. Right again. I was watching a television program called "Conversation" last week, which featured my own publisher, Bennett Cerf; his pretty wife; a bewhiskered British commander and a man named Alfred Kazin. An announcer, Ben Grauer (not pronounced Growler, although I don't see why not), was trying to get the group to talk about present-day American fiction. Phyllis Cerf got in a little plug for me, bless her heart, but the others always got back to how much authors get paid, and my dear publisher apparently is of the opinion that the dough is going the wrong way. I shall take that up *in camera*. The Englishman, who really did have a beard and of course had a pipe, is over here to plug some beverage or other, and by what selective process he was invited to converse about modern American fiction, I cannot say. I am writing to the BBC, making known my availability as a lecturer on Bovril. But the most preposterous statement of the evening, and maybe of the week if you exclude the McCarthy hearings, was uttered by Kazin. Kazin is a man who occasionally turns up in the book review part of the *New Yorker*, where anybody is liable to turn up these days, and I think he is also in the English Department at Columbia. If he isn't, it probably can be arranged. In any event—such as the pole vault or the hammer throw—Mr. Kazin advanced the theory, which he didn't even call a theory, that when an author drops in on his publisher and starts raising the dickens about money, it isn't really the money he's so concerned about. You see, according to Kazin's Law, the author is tired, he is lonely, he has been working so hard on his book that he just wants to talk to somebody. "Kiss me," he practically says. "Mother me. I am a lonely author." The money? Forget it. Let's just chat about the other authors on your list.

Well, that's what the man says. The man that teaches at Columbia and writes reviews for the *New Yorker*. The critic. The opinion-molder.

21.

Within the fortnight past I have performed an act
that is going to have a major effect on a human life.
It was an act as distinguished from something I
wrote. (Naturally I like to think I have great influence on human lives through the power of my
literary efforts, but I am now speaking of an exer-
tion of another kind of influence.) What I did, I
have done before without giving it much thought
and I don't know why I am giving this much
thought, except that in recent months I have been
oftener than not in a contemplative mood; sweet
and sour and neither.

Not to put too much of a strain on the essay style, I was instrumental in getting a young man a job.

I have done that fairly frequently. I have given a young man or young woman the send-in just as I was given the send-in when I was bucking cub reporter. In this case the young man is a senior at a stylish university (not Princeton), the son of a man and woman I knew before he was born. The father is in Europe, so the mother asked me if I would have a talk with the boy, and I did. Then, a few days later, I was having dinner with a friend of mine who had a job for just such a young man. I got employer and candidate together and the boy was signed on. I am perfectly free to feel that my responsibility, if I ever felt one, has ended. The boy is on his own, and so, I may say, is the employer.

And yet I'm not so sure that my responsibility is at an end. This may be a fairly special case, because if I had kept quiet, the boy and the employer never would have known each other. I was more than merely an intermediary. I created the relationship.

The Chinese, I seem to recall from my encyclopedic fund of Oriental erudition, entertain the theory that if you save a man's life you must take care of him for the remainder of his days. I used to think that was preposterous, but then I used to think the Chinese were preposterous. In fact, I used to think people who lived in Ohio were preposterous. My judgments are subject to change without much notice to myself, and I may hang up my stocking next Christmas. Yes, Virginia, I am open to reconviction.

In the present instance I have not saved a young fellow's life, but I may have done better or worse. If he makes good in the new job it will lead into one of the best opportunities in the whole field of endeavor that he has chosen for himself, an opportunity that literally thousands of his contemporaries would give a year's allowance to get. I have no misgivings about his qualifications and eagerness and chance of success. Or, to put it another way, I am not worried about his failing.

I am slightly worried about his making a success and then, say twenty years from now, wishing I had kept my mouth shut. There is practically no chance that I will be around to receive a punch in the nose for what in 1954 seems like an act of kindness, so that isn't worrying me. I suppose what I really worry about is power, and especially any power that one can exercise over anyone else's life. And here we have an example of an exercise of power.

I am in very little danger of being corrupted by power and in no danger at all of being corrupted absolutely, so we can put Lord Acton away for the night. But power worries me, all right, even the relatively minute samples I am able to provide. Thought control, to possess it and employ it, is dangerous stuff, but it isn't thought control I am exam-

ining at this point. I'm just laboring in my own
little Edgartown, which is another way of saying in
only a part of my vineyard, which is my graceful
way of saying I am talking about the power that is
contained in the most casual social intercourse. The
basic social ceremony is the introduction of one human being to another and one of the most casual,
and I wonder if it isn't much too casual, considering
its latent power for good or evil.

I already have taken care of the matter of introducing a young man to an older man who has a job
for him. The fat's in the fire and, if you will excuse
my recording a completely private joke, Pat's on
Fire Island. I functioned as Fate and the boy starts
work in a couple of weeks. Well, what about people
I have introduced who went on to the altar? That
has occurred several times in my career. Years ago
I introduced a man to a girl. Girl a great beauty,
man a newcomer to my sphere of activity. They
danced together and he said to her: "I've always
said I'd know right away the girl I'm going to
marry. Will you marry me?" She did, and when I
say that it didn't turn out well I am exercising so
much restraint that the power of it frightens me. If
I were to put the details in a novel my public
would say I'd been dipping my nose in Stella
Dallas. Out of the kindness of your heart you can
remark that I need not blame myself, that it was a
country club dance and they'd have met anyway.

But I had a hand in it, and better it should have stayed in my pocket. Not all of the introductions I made have produced soap-opera material, but those are the ones you remember, and as I grow older, which is hourly by the minute, I am coming around to the notion that the business of introducing people should be handled with extreme caution and marked "Highly Inflammable," "Restricted," "Classified," "Soft Shoulders," and "Poison." I admit, too, that I am getting stuffy. I have to admit it because I often find myself saying that I now know everybody I want to know. Worse, I have already begun to do a little early fall culling.

You can never know what to expect when you start reading this department, which is at least part of the charm of it. It's part of the charm of it for me, I can tell you, because I don't always know what to expect either. I've already taken a little whack at the evils of power, and that evoluted, as Mr. Stevens would say, out of my thinking out loud about getting a boy a job. Well, what next? What for instance would you think might come out of a cigarette case? You might come right back at me: "Cigarettes!" But you haven't got my cigarette case, the one John Steinbeck gave me. Why John Steinbeck gave me a cigarette case is quite a story in itself, which will have to be withheld at this time. Enough to say that I have the case and to tell you what he had engraved in it: "The lonely mind of one man is the only creative organ in the world and any force which interferes with its free function is the Enemy." (There's more, but it is personal and I don't quite know you well enough.) What made me think of the inscription while I was free-wheeling along about jobs and introductions? Well, I've gone back and traced the thoughts, so how about if you give it a try? There's a connection, all right, and if you've stuck with me this far you may be able to figure it out without much trouble.

22.

It is not one bit too early to start thinking about what reading you are going to postpone this summer. Next week we'll be in June, with its weddings and graduations and college reunions to occupy so much of one's time. The sanctioned lusts of last December will be getting finalized, as Senator Mundt loves to say; the sweet girl graduates (and the sour ones) will be hearing about their Fulbrights; and the gay blades of other years will be limping back to the best old place of all (Southern Methodist).

Then, before you know it, business will be suspended while a check is made on the standings in the American and National Leagues, Junior will be getting a first-degree burn from picking up a live sparkler (silly little jerk that he is), and Bastille Day will be almost upon us. Let us therefore be forehanded and rough out some plans now for those annual struggles of the intellect known as catching up on worth-while books.

If I can be of any help I'll be only too glad. I say in all modesty that I am somewhat of an authority on neglected reading, having neglected most of the greatest books in literature over a period of forty-five years, or ever since I learned to read. In that time I have managed to create a set of rules and traditions that apply to the neglecting of great books.

I will not go so far as to say they are hard and fast rules, because I never knew what hard and fast rules means. It probably is one of your coursing terms and has to do with the going. In any event the term is an obscure one, and while I may not always know what I am talking about, I do always know what I am saying.

First on everyone's Neglected list is, of course, *War and Peace*. It is a durable work, durable in this respect: I have carried it on my Neglected list for more than thirty years and, like all classics, it is sure to outlast me. It occupies a place of prominence in the bookshelf at Dunrovin, my summer cottage, and it deserves more than a passing mention for the rather interesting excuses I have invented to neglect it. Of the millions of people who have *War and Peace* on their Neglected list, I may have one excuse that is unique: a few years ago I had made my usual resolution to wrestle with the book, in part shamed into the resolution by the girl I love, who actually had finished the book and was urging me to follow suit. But one day I looked out upon the beach in front of my next-door neighbor's and I recognized a man whom I had known slightly for several years. That cooked *War and Peace* for that summer. Why read the book when I could offer drinks to a cousin of Leo Tolstoy's?

So far as I can testify, no cousin of Adolf Hitler's is or has been a visitor in my neighborhood, but I have kept *Mein Kampf* in a practically untouched state on my shelves, and the same goes for *Das Kapital.* Where I go in the summer you are more likely to encounter admirers of Hitler than of Marx, but since I am an admirer of neither and found the latter as baffling as *Finnegans Wake,* I compromised by neglecting both, and incidentally *Finnegans Wake* as well.

I must seem a rare bird to the local pharmacists, who in eighteen years have not had to fill more than two prescriptions for sleeping pills for me. They know me to be an author and therefore a queer duck in the duck country, but to them the strangest thing about me is, I am sure, the fact that I buy no barbiturics although I belong to a profession that con-

sumes them like jujubes. What my chemist does
not know is that at home I keep within easy bedside
reach a copy of *The Way of All Flesh* and one of
The American Senator. Sandman comes almost the
minute I adjust the lamp and perch one of those
novels on my abdomen. For stubborn cases of in-
somnia, following days when the rain has kept me
off the golf course, almost any volume of verse will
do the trick. Much more effective than a hot bath,
and makes me less liable to contract a cold. (Actually don't contract a cold, I expand it.)

This might seem like a glorious opportunity to put
some of my contemporaries in their place by enu-
merating authors who can send me to dreamland
with two short paragraphs. Unfortunately, I gave the
management my vow of truth and consequently I
am unable in that way to insult my unfavorite authors. It would not be the truth for me to say that
some of those dunderheaded incompetents can put
me to sleep. What they do, really, is make me so
angry that I throw their books across the room, usually knock down a lamp, and get so wide awake that
only a diligent study of the *Congressional Record*
can calm me down.

Also, I cannot claim that I would have their books
in my house in the first place, and in this essay I
was taking up the Neglected, not the Ignored. Nor
do I in this study mean to include authors who
merely bore me. My object, may I remind you, was

to discuss books that I intend to read, a very different matter from a discussion of books that I never intend to read. There is one author, for instance, whom I consider to be not good enough to be instructive and not bad enough to be entertaining, and since as a pro I try to read for instruction or entertainment, I pass him up.

Nor do I want you to think that it is merciful sleep alone that keeps me from making a sizable dent in the list of Neglected books. I may start the afternoon with a copy of *Vanity Fair* on my lap, then before I can get rolling, some weary traveler breaks the journey to East Hampton with a visit to my liquor closet. On occasion such a visit has been known to wind up at the Cruiser Club at four the next morning, with my caller only ten miles closer to East Hampton and me no closer to Becky Sharp. As a new member of Abstainers Acknowledged, I may not be able this summer to produce the same conditions, but I can find more excuses for not finishing a great book than Stringfellow Barr can for limiting his list to a hundred.

There is golf, a pastime which as I play it should hold no more charm than the Catherine wheel, the iron maiden, or Russian roulette. Not only does it keep me from reading the great books; it keeps sending me back to another book called *Golf After 40* which fascinates me, all right, but apparently had so little fascination for other players that I had to advertise for it. And now that I have slimmed down to a boyish 190, *Golf After 40,* which was composed for men who had some difficulty swinging around their own porches, no longer is quite so useful. But my new reedy figure will not cause me to inter my schnoz in *Letters of a Young Poet.*

Ah, there are so many distractions. There's always a ball game, afternoon and evening, Dodgers and Yanks. There's the ritual known as Going for the Mail and Papers, with its subtleties of social intercourse such as how cordially to nod to whom, how long to engage in conversation with the local peace officers, what lengths to go to in brushing off pests, and things like that. And of course there's always a little work to do around the house, shoes to shine, brasses to rub, bills to throw away, typewriter ribbons to change, publishers to needle, collect.

I suppose the best excuse, at least for an author, is in the unanswerable question: Would Thackeray read me?

23.

Why, I even wrote a piece for *Flair,* for heaven's sake.

This admission, or boast, as you prefer, is made as part of a soul-searching I did the other day. The occasion, not a notable one, was the reading of a kind of letter that I can expect about ten times a year. Young man or young woman writes to ask how I got in the writing game and what I did when I got in. I long since have given up answering such letters in detail, not because I am an old stuffy (although I am), but because I have found that the little dears don't really care.

You reply in detail, a correspondence ensues, then one day you answer the doorbell and Charlie Bismuth is there, bummed his way from Momence, Illinois, and would like you to call up Harry Luce and Raoul Fleischmann and tell them to give Charlie a job. He won't believe it when I protest that a letter from me to *Time* or *The New Yorker* would be the buss of oblivion. He has a fourth dollop of my bourbon and feels free to tell me that I am a big phony and Glenway Wescott can write rings around me. If the visitor happens to be of the female persuasion it usually takes five of my bourbons and it's Carson McCullers that I ought to take lessons from, but there is no essential difference that I can see. Either way, I get the blues, and I'm just too mean to cry.

But I started to say I wrote a piece for *Flair*. You remember *Flair*. If you don't remember *Flair*, you may at least have used an expression I invented for my piece: Expense Account Society. Luce's picture book waited for what they regarded as a decent interval and then rewrote my *Flair* piece, so you may have read about Expense Account Society in Luce's picture book. I think it was rather naughty of old Luce, no matter how far he felt he was being driven by the Cowles interests.

It is my observation that what Clare has done, Fleur can do. Mrs. Luce as Mrs. Brokaw took hold of a real classy magazine called *Vanity Fair,* and in practically no time it disappeared from view. Mrs.

Cowles did not just take a property in being; she went to the great trouble of originating a magazine and then made it disappear. *Flair* had a lot of things wrong with it; in the old Irish phrase, it was as queer as Dick's hatband (no reference to Dick Whitney and his Porcellian colors).

You would be reading an article on the one perfect rose and all of a sudden your thumb would be sticking out of the page. Kind ladies have been telling me for years that I have nice hands, but I have no illusions about my thumbs. I would not be without them, understand, but I do not think they contribute anything to the prose style of an article on the one perfect rose. There is this to be said in Mrs. Cowles' favor: she exterminated a magazine that asked for it. *Vanity Fair* deserved to remain.

I wrote a pretty good piece for *Vanity Fair*. Fiction. I also wrote a short story for the *Brooklyn Daily Eagle Magazine*, excellent piece, ahead of its time. Where else have I appeared? Well, I never sent a story to *Rob Wagner's Script*, but I got stuck for two stories in a magazine called *Carnival*. Somewhere in this room—but try and find them—are two stock certificates in payment of one of the *Carnival* stories, and if I ever get around to it, I'm going to have them matted and framed. Any near-sighted person will assume that they are diplomas or citations, and any Charlie Bismuth will hurry back to Momence and the job in Dad's groover factory.

In an extremely active career I once wrote for an
if-money publication that was being brought along
by two men named Fred Palmer and Malcolm
Ross. My recollection is that it was called *Today
—in New York,* but I won't swear to it. I know that
years later, when I ran into Palmer in Grand Cen-
tral, I had too much native tact to speak of the paper at all.

When the starry-eyed ask me if I ever wrote for
Hearst, I say "You're damn right I did." I worked
for Reid when I was rooting for Al Smith and the
Herald Trib was against him, which made me precisely as much a hypocrite as I was later when I did
jobs for Hearst during his anti-F.D.R. days. I know
three of the Hearst sons and never a cross word between us, although they are in no doubt as to my
politics. I'll "work for Hearst" any time the price
and the assignment are right, and I've never had to
eat with George Sokolsky. Have you? Don't tell me
about it.

Let me see where else this golden by-line has appeared. During one miserable transition I was man-
aging editor of a curious publication that I suspect
existed to keep the owner's younger brother out of
trouble. Idle hands, you know. Junior—he wasn't
actually Junior, but I'll call him that—knew slightly
more about publishing than does our toy poodle, but
I'm pretty sure I could give the poodle a short
course, say two weeks, and he'd graduate higher

than Junior. Of one thing I am positive: the dog has better manners. I quit the job for several reasons, prominent among them being Junior's schoolgirlish habit of opening all mail, even or especially mail addressed to me in feminine handwriting. I was planning a little practical joke on Junior, but I grew weary of him and the paper and the town before I could execute the lesson. One of the regrets of my life is that I didn't take a commission I was offered, with which I'd have ranked Junior by two full stripes and in the same area. Do you think I made a mistake? I think I made a mistake.

You can find an article on the martini cocktail in a magazine called *For Men*, but first you have to find *For Men*. I wrote that one in an agent's office while waiting for the agent to disengage himself from the telephone and join me in a mart. I sold a short story to *The Strand*, which had been around a long time but now reposes, along with *For Men* and *Flair*, in Magazine Heaven. It may have occurred to you, as it certainly has to me, that my presence in a publication does not guarantee success.

However, I've written for Luce and *The New Yorker*, *Collier's*, *The Saturday Evening Post*, *The New York Times*, the *Trib*, International News Service, *Cosmopolitan*, *Good Housekeeping*, and the *Hampton Chronicle*, all of which are still around, and I just wrote a piece for *The Fire Islander*, a brand-new journal that I haven't killed yet. If I really felt that I possessed some diabolical power I'd bombard certain publications, not excluding all those mentioned above, with manuscripts, until I achieved my fiendish purpose. But I have been so cautious in the exercise of the power of the printed word that restraint has become a habit with me, Dr. Canby to the contrary. I just go on doing the best I can with what I got and I don't worry about the power or influence or lack of same, and where the stuff appears doesn't make much difference so long as the groceries appear. In one year I had the somewhat transvestite experience of appearing in both *Esquire* and *Harper's Bazaar,* and yet I remain the simple peasant.

24.

It must have been an exhausting week for Mado, or at least a busy one. I should perhaps explain now, because I'm going to have to sooner or later, that Mado, Madeline Hurlock, is the present Mrs. Robert E. Sherwood. Before that she was Mrs. Marc Connelly, and if you were hitting your New York dailies with any regularity you saw that Connelly got conked and Sherwood also did a little public bleeding, in the strictly metaphorical sense.

Connelly was walking along the street when a wicker chair arrived, as from heaven, and ricocheted off Marc's skull on its (the chair's) way to

the sidewalk. Sherwood, at the annual jamboree of
the Institute of Arts and Letters, said, among other
things, that Benjamin Franklin's aspirations for liberty and the rights of man are so out of tune with
the temper of the present as to seem downright sub-
versive. If you think that last statement doesn't
sound like me, you are right; it is a quote from *The
New York Times*. It must, as I say, have been a
crowded week for Mrs. Sherwood, but I want you
to draw no inferences from the fact that the day
after Connelly stopped the furniture, the Sherwoods
sailed for Europe. Such inferences would be guilt by
association.

You see, don't you, that all I am doing is to remind the nubile among my readers that marriage to
an author has its interesting moments as well as its
dull ones. I could rest my case on the fact that as
fascinating a woman as Madeline Hurlock has married two prominent playwrights and in the second,
or Sherwood, instance has remained wife to him for
almost twenty years. But I can't help further remind-
ing my Radcliffe and Rider public that life with an
author need not be merely a state in which the girl
must endure the husband's brooding, his financial
instability, his moping, his complaining, his inability
to take care of fuses, his trips to nowhere, his boast-
ing of his superiority over other authors, and his
firm belief in his irresistibility to other women. Before the lawyers come I hasten to say that I have

made that list of auctorial habits without even the slightest reference to my files on Sherwood and Connelly. For all I know—Sherwood and Connelly can go down in history as model husbands. So, Sweetie, don't jilt the guy just because he craves to be a writer. Find some other reason, and the chances are you can.

I find it not at all difficult to spurn Mr. Sherwood's ideas as reported in the press. He says, if our 43rd Street neighbor quotes him accurately, that that country (meaning this country), is in a "phase in which suspicion automatically attaches itself to the philosopher, the poet, the artist, the scientist, the teacher—even the free-thinking preacher—to anyone who is contaminated with that damning word 'intellectual'."

Well, let's have a look at that. A few years ago Charles A. Beard, the historian, and a member of the Institute of which Sherwood and Connelly are and were conspicuous members, had taken a political position that was antipodally removed from the politics that Sherwood (and Connelly) believed in. Was Beard drummed out of the Institute? Of course he wasn't. To the best of my knowledge, the only thing that happened was that Lewis Mumford resigned in protest against Beard's utterances. One man, an intellectual, bowed out as a gesture of disapproval of another intellectual's beliefs. That's inside the Institute.

I am better qualified to report on conditions on the outside. I would not go so far as to call myself an intellectual, because I don't think a man ought to call himself an intellectual any more than he ought to call himself handsome. But I am an artist, and I am a liberal. I am a struggling artist and an avowed liberal, who supported many of the things Sherwood was for, and opposed practically everything Sherwood was against. If suspicion has attached to me because I am an artist and a liberal, what of it?

Suspicion of what, and by whom? Suspicion of communism? Suspicion of fascism? If I am suspected of communism I can point out that practically the only people who have called me an intellectual are the thought-controllers in the Eastern Zone of Germany, where my books are banned. And if I am suspected of fascism, the fascists should be told about a member they don't know about.

Now I don't like McCarthy, but my not liking McCarthy doesn't automatically make me like Stevens. I reserve certain rights, one of them being the right to discriminate between what I think is good and what I think isn't, and as Mr. Welch would say, this tiny, this pitifully small voice must be raised, however ineffectually, in the forlorn little hope that one or two kindly folk would listen while O'Hara timidly calls their attention to the fact that less than a year ago, Mr. Chairman, McCarthy and Stevens were Joe and Bob. To return to my own style, I don't believe either man changed. They merely disagreed.

Such a statement by me can provoke the wrath of both sides to the current controversy, but surely Sherwood (and Connelly) would rush to my defense if there were any effort to shut my mouth. Not to do so would be unthinkable, if I followed Sherwood's reasoning, for he also said: "Whenever we find ourselves in a phase which involves even the suspicion of a threat to intellectual freedom and integrity, then it is time for the members of the Academy and this Institute to make themselves heard in protest—loud protest."

There will be a time lapse between this writing and its appearance in print, so Connelly may have taken that opportunity to correct me and other readers of *The New York Times,* but he made a remarkable comment when the chair hit him. "I always knew children were anti-social," he said, according to the *Times,* "but children on the West Side are savages."

When he got home, with his head swaddled in gauze, he said: "I pity the poor kids who did it. They may feel a lot worse than I unless they're complete psychopaths."

And when neighbors and strangers came to his aid, he said, they made him feel "the human race is made up of very nice people."

The latter two statements sound more like Connelly of the Institute, the—no suspicion attached

—intellectual. But as of this writing, he probably is on the hook with the West Side Association for that first reaction. I think he may even be hearing from the East Side.

But he won't be hearing from me, for I am a liberal. If I had my skull bones tapped in like circumstances, no newspaper in the country could have printed my remarks. I commend Connelly for his restraint.

However, I do urge my readers to consider the fact that so civilized a man as Connelly did to some extent lose control, as quoted. Even the East Side, even Connelly, is not so far removed from the savage.

25.

If you want to touch on a touchy subject, rub your manual appendages over Plagiarism, from *plagiarius,* kidnapper; and from the Greek *plagios,* oblique, crooked. How sharper than a serpent's tooth is the touchy subject Plagiarism, how rougher than the armor in which the armadillo dillows, and how thick-skinned the characters who are guilty of plagiarizing. So it doesn't make much difference to them. The only thing they are sensitive to is the slap, as in slapping them with a law suit. But what a bother; and money you make that way never did anybody any good, although I'd sometimes like to put that kind of money to the test.

If my solicitors will arrange to win me $400,000 in a plagiarism action I shall be most happy to submit myself to the experiment of determining how little good that kind of dough can do. I have always liked $400,000, admiring it from afar as a substantial sum without the vulgarity that somehow attaches to the possession of a million. (I'll throw away my Eton collar and go vulgar for a million, too.) The trouble is—and now I am being frightfully serious—if you sue for plagiarism, and win, you look a little like a jerk and a sorehead. If you sue and lose—oh, boy!

I got off on this kick because the night before last I was studying the offering on the "Late Late Show" and I wasn't studying it very long before a character of mine came to life. Some decades ago I grew weary of the department in the *Reader's Digest* called My Most Unforgettable Character, or something to that effect. The M. U. C. usually was an old colored mammy who for years had been working secretly in her makeshift laboratory out back and had developed a cure for penicillin; or it was a town drunk who in his youth had swum the English Channel with anvils instead of flippers tied to his ankles; or it was Mother. In any case, the authors almost uniformly adopted an attitude so patronizing that I wanted to scream, and because I knew many of the authors I frequently did scream: "Who the hell are you to patronize anybody!"

In due course I wrote a satire of the M. U. C. series and sold it to Ross's Folly. I called it "Life Among These Unforgettable Characters" thus announcing not too subtly that I was kidding the *Digest*. It was a pretty funny piece, and one of the funniest things about it was that a man named Gerald W. Johnson, an editorial writer, took it very seriously and went into a big thing about geriatrics. My unforgettable character became truly unforgettable at least to the scenarists of that "Late Late Show" movie. My invention was an irascible but hateful old gent who ran a filling station in the desert, compelled the customers to wait on themselves and insisted on their making change. The scenarists liked him so much that they opened the picture with him.

Now what do you do in a case like that? It was an obvious and unmistakable theft, and the scenarists (maybe there was only one; I didn't see the screen credits) had taken money for their script which was in part based on an invention of mine. If they signed the standard writer's contract with the producing company, and I must assume they did, they promised, hope to die, that they would do original work, and they also agreed to some kind of waiver that has for its purpose the protection of the producers, although I don't believe that paragraph stands up in law. What kind of no-good bums, besides no-good, will see a character in a magazine piece or a

"You mean *My Friend Flicka,* by Mary O'Hara." Fill
in your own dialogue, I have work to do.)

Well, to go back to Paragraph I, Title I, Section I,
my larcenous union of titles belonging to Truman
Capote and James T. Farrell would have made a
pretty, though wordy, heading for my comment on
a book I have been giving house room. It is called
Persona Grata, and the author billing is "By Cecil
Beaton and Kenneth Tynan." The world of Cecil
Beaton is certainly one I never made, either in the
creational or the invitational sense of the word. Mr.
Beaton is remembered by me for two things: He
called Clare Boothe Luce "drenchingly lovely," which
I have always regarded as the most dubious compli-
ment a woman ever got. His other accomplishment
(aside, that is, from his unquestionably good photog-
raphy) was a questionable gesture he made on the
cover of some magazine, and I don't even remember
that very well. In a *découpage* or something of the
sort he snuck in naughty little comments that had the
Vogue-El Morocco set twittering like as if Mona Williams appeared at Quaglino's in levis. That, as the
police say, is my sheet on C. Beaton. Mr. Tynan is
known to me only as a young Londoner who, according to Richard Watts, Jr., is the most brilliant of the
English drama critics. I cannot give Watts an argu-
ment, since I am unacquainted with Tynan's stuff
other than what I have seen in *Persona Grata.* Brilliant I suppose is the word for the text he has supplied

for Beaton's pictures, although for the benefit of my friend Charles Poore I am strongly tempted to say that Tynan is coruscating on thin ice.

I am fascinated by the rich and how they live, and I go with them every chance I get. But once again I have to confess to snobbishness. Those rich who continue to be designated as Mayfair do not fascinate me, and they remain other voices in other rooms. I am not going to expose the rug over my lungs and claim membership in The Toughies. I never asked to be put up there. But on the occasions when I have been in those other rooms, listening to those other voices—and believe me, I listen, for I never have much to say—I am uncomfortable, ill at ease, and glad to get out without knocking over the Sèvres.

When I am not uncomfortable, I am bored. The women are mostly thin and ugly or fat and ugly, the men are mostly thin and pretty or fat and menacing. They are all conformists to The Different and consequently in a group they are precisely what they think they're not: they are conventional, in their way as conventional as a gathering of Kiwanians or Sheet Metal Workers or alumni of Folsom. And as obvious as my comment on their conventionalism is the fact that among them are scads of no-talent joes who belong in those rooms for no other reason than that they, too, had trouble with Nursie at a tender age.

A darling man named Joe Brooks, who died last year, once remarked that you never know the holes

in the lining of the other fellow's coat. That's one of
the reasons I prefer to be in the company of those
rich who, you might say, start conventional. The men
and women whose fathers, at least, lived on the
income of their income, the people who can buy anything but don't. You see a large band of them assem-
bling at a wedding, for instance, and there is a
wholesale display of politeness, a fair uniformity of
attire among the men, and an exhibition of fashion
among the women. You observe that they are clean,
that they have appetites for food and drink, that they
love sport or despise it. That's the big picture. If you,
like me, are an outsider, for you they start conventional. But then you see a little more of them and then
still a little more, and then you begin to see the holes
in the lining. Pretty soon you realize that the moths
have been really industrious—and it's time you got so
yourself, if you are a novelist.

For twenty years, off and on, I have been gawking
and listening and comparing the results with my find-
ings after a like period of study of small-town country-
club life. There is a difference. The small town, like
my invention Gibbsville, has it all; the entrenched,
the strivers, the climbers, the rebellious. But the big
town, by which I mean the Boston–Providence–New
York–Philadelphia–Wilmington–Baltimore group, offer many more of the entrenched, the striving, the
climbing and the rebelling to choose from. And of
course they're richer. What is particularly nice is that

they don't produce novelists. Aside from Louis Auchincloss, whose work I know only from review quotes, I can't think of any Insider who has dared to risk ostracism by slipping out messages to the Outside.

Oddly enough, the Beaton set and the Beacon Hill billies have this in common: they both are tough to write about, or at least they are to me. The Beatonians do not interest me except as minor characters in a book or a play, and therefore are not easy to make interesting. The Auchinclossers do interest me, and I have abundant information on their habits and their tribal customs, but they interest me so much that it's hard for me to know when to stop. I do know when to stop this piece. Right now.

27.

And now, friends and others, we part company. By agreement with the management, made six months ago, Smilin' Jack, the All-American Boy, puts the hats and the rabbits and the wand back in the box. In plain language, with this installment *Sweet & Sour* comes to an end.

In the very first paragraph of the very first piece, back on December 27, 1953, I said that the existence of this column is all the proof you need that anybody can get a job in Trenton if he tries long enough. Now I wish to make another statement, not an original one, but a major one. It is, simply: Trenton Makes—

the World Takes. In this case, the Trenton product is a book, a collection of these pieces which will be published in the fall. Would there be any objection if I inserted the intelligence that the book will be called—surprise!—*Sweet & Sour*, and it will be published by Random House? It will be given away free with every purchase of a genuine pearl necklace at Cartier's, or, if you prefer, and if present negotiations are successfully concluded, with every fifteen-year subscription to this newspaper. If you decide that you'd rather buy the book outright, the customary arrangements can be made with your bookseller. At this early date I am unable to announce the retail price of the collection, because I don't know what it will be. (Oh, I'd tell you if I knew.) But as a slight tickle to your eleemosynary instinct you should know that I get a straight 15 percent royalty from my publishers. In the barren language of commerce, if you fork over $3.00 for this little honey of a tome, I will collect 45 cents. If you are concerned about authors' getting rich and lazy, I probably don't have to remind you that it takes an awful lot of 45 centses to do me any harm. I won't say that I am only one jump ahead of the sheriff, but I wouldn't have to strain myself if I felt like reaching out to touch Silver's withers.

It will be fun to have a book out again. If you've had the experience I suggest you flip back a few pages and see what's been going on in Hackettstown;

but if you've never had a book published I can tell you that there's nothing like it. Seems to me I did cover this ground pretty thoroughly a couple of months ago, but I may have left out some details. The other day, and just to show how fast things can move in the lit'ry world, I received the artist's sketch of the jacket. The book is not yet in type, but already an artist has submitted, and I have okayed, the plan for the dust cover. Mighty good-looking. Attractive and effective, I told Cerf, in the optimistic mood you're always in at this stage of publication. I placed the sketch, which is done on Bristol board, at various locations in my living room, trying it out on the endless stream of people who come to me for guidance, counsel, and friendship and to deliver the eggs. I was hoping to nab the parcel-post man because he is a highly literate, well-spoken fellow, but nobody sent me anything this week. The verdict, however, was that the jacket is eye-catching. It is striped, like a tennis blazer that my mother used to wear before she gave me to a waiting world. I am color-blind for certain colors, so I have had to rely on the good taste and common sense of artist and publisher in that respect.

This will be the third book I have had published since moving to Mercer County, and my, how the time has flown. And my, how sometimes it has dragged. I know that these pieces are sometimes read by young people who are thinking of making writing a career, so I will tell them one thing about the pieces: all but two were written during the time of the greatest tragedy that has happened in my life, really the only tragedy. Nobody can survive two tragedies. Of that I shall say no more, but I reluctantly admit that much because the pieces have been generally in a frivolous tone and I want the young to realize that writing is, among other things, an act, like a vaudeville act. If you are a pro, you keep going. If you are not a pro, you get the hell out. For that reason, I am grateful for this job. I could not have worked on a novel or a play, but these essays—and that's what they are, even though you may be accustomed to Addison—were just the right kind of work to have to do.

For the interested, and since this is a sort of valedictory, and it's June, I shall do a little class history, class-prophecy type of wordage. Somewhere back there I must have said that I am learning all the time. If I didn't say it I'm surprised, because I do say it all the time. I may have said it this way: that I believe an author should try everything. Well, I tried writing a weekly column on an excellent book page, and have done it to my own satisfaction. It did not turn out to be a booksy column, but I don't think the management ever expected any such thing from this quarter. In another life I did a weekly column on entertainment, just as I am now doing a fortnightly department in the same field. For the im-

mediate future, I am returning, as it were, to one
of my first loves, the Thutta. But big. I have three
plays making the rounds of the managers. I am
going to continue writing plays until I have three
successes. I am going to write for television until
I have produced three successful ones. Next year I
am going to have another novel for sale. Since I have
been cautioned not to renew acquaintance with my
dear old friend Scotch whiskey, and since by success
I also mean a financial success, I should have, within
the next two years, ample time to go back to work
on my narrative poem. That will be a financial and
time loss, but if I still have some dough left over, I
am going to try to get a commission to write the
libretto of an opera, an original American opera. My
dependent is already a little past the age when I
would enjoy writing a children's book for her, a project I once considered seriously. I used to make up
stories for her. I had to stop though, and do you know
why? Rather interesting, why. The stories were about
a maiden lady and her cat and her friend the telephone operator and the animals that lived near the
maiden lady's house. The trouble was, the stories
were laid in Kenya, near Nairobi (where of course
I've never been), and when the Mau Mau ruckus
started and all those pictures appeared in the magazines, the illusion was broken and the stories ceased
to interest my audience. So—no children's book. I
wrote (and illustrated) dozens of poems for that

special section of my public, but they were private and personal, not for publication—and probably not poetry. But I tried, and they were well received at the time.

As a last word I have one statement to make about the management. In thirty years of earning my living at my typewriter I never have enjoyed such complete freedom from what is called pencil-editing. Some of the things I wrote must have given them sharp pains, but they ran them. If you don't think that makes an author happy—well, you know it does make an author happy.

Thank you.

ABOUT THE AUTHOR

John O'Hara's first novel, *Appointment in Samarra*, was published in 1934. Ever since its appearance he has been a major figure on the American literary scene and has been on intimate terms with publishers, authors and critics.

Son of a doctor and the eldest of eight children, Mr. O'Hara was born in Pottsville, Pennsylvania, in 1905. After graduation from Niagara Prep School, he worked as a ship steward, railway freight clerk, gas-meter reader, amusement-park guard, soda clerk and press agent. For a time he was secretary to the late Heywood Broun.

O'Hara's career as a reporter was equally varied. He worked first for two Pennsylvania papers and then for three in New York, where he covered everything from sports to religion. He also was on the staff of *Newsweek* and *Time*.

His two previous novels were *A Rage to Live* (1949) and *The Farmers Hotel* (1951). He was also the author of the smash-hit musical comedy, *Pal Joey*, for which Lorenz Hart wrote the lyrics and Richard Rodgers the musical score. His column, "Appointment with O'Hara," is now a regular feature in *Collier's* magazine. Mr. O'Hara lives in Princeton, New Jersey.